Understanding

Hip and Knee Arthritis Surgery

Mr Richard Villar

Published by Family Doctor Publications Limited
in association with the British Medical Association

IMPORTANT

This book is intended not as a substitute for personal medical advice but as a supplement to that advice for the patient who wishes to understand more about his or her condition.

Before taking any form of treatment
YOU SHOULD ALWAYS CONSULT YOUR MEDICAL PRACTITIONER.

In particular (without limit) you should note that advances in medical science occur rapidly and some information about drugs and treatment contained in this booklet may very soon be out of date.

© Family Doctor Publications 2000–2008
Updated 2002, 2003, 2005, 2008

Family Doctor Publications, PO Box 4664, Poole, Dorset BH15 1NN

ISBN-13: 978 1 903474 44 0
ISBN-10: 1 903474 44 2

Contents

About the author

Mr Richard Villar, MS, FRCS is a Consultant Orthopaedic Surgeon in Cambridge and a specialist in hip and knee surgery. He researches and lectures extensively in these fields and has a particular interest in musculoskeletal transplantation and arthroscopic (keyhole) surgery of the hip joint.

Introduction

Arthritis

Arthritis has existed for thousands of years. There are about 200 types that can affect all ages, although the most common are osteoarthritis and rheumatoid arthritis. It was only in the twentieth century that the two were recognised as different. Indeed, as recently as the eighteenth century all forms of arthritis were thought to be caused by gout.

Human beings are not alone in developing arthritis. Animals can also suffer from it, and ancient humans also developed it. Over 50 per cent of the population have arthritis in one or more of their joints. By the time you are 75 years old, there is an 85 per cent chance that you will have developed arthritis somewhere, particularly in the larger joints such as the hip or knee.

As arthritis is so common it is a major concern to the whole population. Not only does it affect the individual who has developed the disease, but it also affects relatives, friends, work colleagues and others, who must provide support for those who have it. Quality of life plummets, income can fall and treatment is regularly needed.

The human skeleton

The human skeleton is able to articulate so well because it has many joints. These tend to degenerate over time and can cause pain and discomfort.

BONES

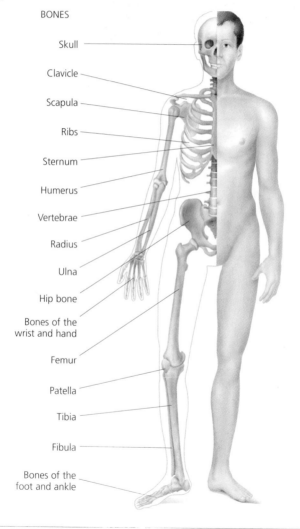

- Skull
- Clavicle
- Scapula
- Ribs
- Sternum
- Humerus
- Vertebrae
- Radius
- Ulna
- Hip bone
- Bones of the wrist and hand
- Femur
- Patella
- Tibia
- Fibula
- Bones of the foot and ankle

Treating arthritis

Treatment can be either medical, with the provision of drugs and other non-invasive therapies, or surgical. The purpose of this book is to look at the various surgical solutions. Much of an orthopaedic surgeon's work in the modern era concerns the surgery of arthritis.

The two most common joints affected are the hip and the knee, both being major weight-bearing joints which for a long period take the knocks and thumps of everyday life. Surgical solutions can take many forms. Some are widely performed, whereas others are to be found only in specialist centres.

Despite the frequency of surgery, there are few places a patient may learn about the relative merits and disadvantages of surgery. This book aims to fill that gap.

KEY POINTS

- Over 50 per cent of the population have arthritis in one or more of their joints

- By the age of 75, there is an 85 per cent chance that you will have developed arthritis somewhere

- Treatment of arthritis can be either medical or surgical

- The two most common joints affected are the hip and the knee

Hips and knees – what they look like and how they work

The hip and knee joints

At each end of the long thigh bone (femur) there is a large weight-bearing joint. At the bottom is the knee and at the top is the hip. Although both joints are essential for walking, each looks totally different.

Hips

Each hip is a ball-and-socket joint. At the top end of the femur is the rounded femoral head that lies in the spherical hip socket (acetabulum).

To enable the joint to move with limited friction, the surfaces that lie against each other (articulating surfaces) are covered with gristle (articular cartilage). The gristle is lubricated by a tiny quantity of a yellowish fluid (synovial fluid), allowing the joint to move with less friction than even a skate on ice.

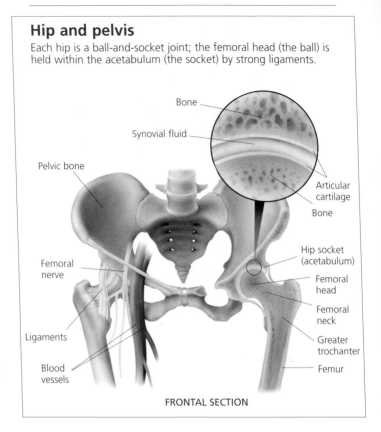

Hip and pelvis

Each hip is a ball-and-socket joint; the femoral head (the ball) is held within the acetabulum (the socket) by strong ligaments.

Bone

Synovial fluid

Pelvic bone

Articular cartilage

Bone

Femoral nerve

Hip socket (acetabulum)

Femoral head

Femoral neck

Ligaments

Greater trochanter

Blood vessels

Femur

FRONTAL SECTION

The femoral head is connected to the main shaft of the femur by a firm bridge of bone called the femoral neck. When elderly people fracture their hip joints, it is actually the femoral neck that is damaged.

At the junction of the femoral neck and the femoral shaft is a large bony protrusion called the greater trochanter. This is the hard lump of bone that can be felt on the outside of the hip and to which most people point when asked to indicate their own hip joint. In fact, the greater trochanter is not the hip joint at all, but it is connected to the hip joint by the femoral head and neck.

The femoral head is kept within the acetabulum by strong ligaments. If these ligaments are divided (for example, at surgery) or ruptured (for example, in a car accident) then the hip can dislocate.

Dislocation can damage the blood supply to the femoral head by tearing the blood vessels, and the poor blood flow that results can, in turn, lead to the development of arthritis in later years.

Surrounding the hip joint are three major nerves: the femoral nerve, the sciatic nerve and the obturator nerve. These nerves transport nerve impulses back and forth from the hip, groin and lower limbs to the brain through the spinal cord, so that movement can be controlled and sensations felt. These nerves are, in turn, surrounded by blood vessels and major muscles.

The most powerful muscles supporting the hip joint are the three muscles known as glutei (gluteus maximus, gluteus medius and gluteus minimus) behind and the rectus femoris and iliopsoas muscles in front. If the glutei weaken, as happens when arthritis progresses, then a patient begins to limp.

The hip joint develops in the embryo after only eight weeks in the womb. Bones do not initially appear in bony form at all, but start as cartilage (firm, jelly-like substance) and then gradually turn into bone (hard substance filled with calcium). This process is known as ossification, and involves the removal of cartilage, which is replaced by calcium-rich bone, laid down by special bone-producing cells.

The centres of most bones become ossified in childhood, but the ends remain undeveloped till puberty to leave room for growth. At some stage between the ages of 15 and 25 years the hip joint becomes fully developed and growth in that area ceases.

As people grow older, so their bones can become thinner, and in certain circumstances smaller. This is known as osteoporosis, a form of bone weakening that can lead to fractures, particularly of the hip, wrist and spine. Osteoporosis is different to osteoarthritis, though the two terms are often confused.

Knees

The knee is a very complex joint, formed by three bones: the shin bone (tibia), thigh bone (femur) and kneecap (patella). The fibula is near to the knee joint but does not specifically form part of it.

The knee is a hinge joint, that is, it mostly allows movement in a single plane, like the hinge of a door, although some rotation is possible.

The lower end of the femur (thigh bone) is rounded to form the femoral condyles. The upper end of the tibia (shin bone) is flattened to form the tibial plateau. Logically, it seems a wonder that a joint of this shape can provide balance at all, but it does do so with the support of strong ligaments, which connect the lower femur to the upper tibia.

The ligaments of the knee include the collateral ligaments at each side and the cruciate ligaments in the centre of the joint. The cruciates, particularly the anterior cruciate ligament, are the structures so frequently relied upon, and damaged, by athletes.

On the front of the knee lies the patella (kneecap). This lies on the front of the lower femur, forming a joint called the patellofemoral joint. Injuries and diseases of this joint are a frequent cause of pain.

Knee joint

The knee is a hinge joint that mostly allows movement in one plane, like the hinge of a door, although some rotation is possible.

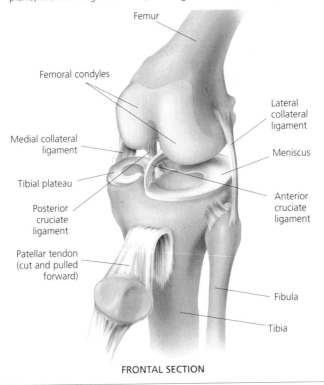

Femur

Femoral condyles

Lateral collateral ligament

Medial collateral ligament

Meniscus

Tibial plateau

Posterior cruciate ligament

Anterior cruciate ligament

Patellar tendon (cut and pulled forward)

Fibula

Tibia

FRONTAL SECTION

At the top end of the kneecap is attached the quadriceps muscle (the large bulky muscle in front of the thigh) and at the lower end is a tendon that inserts into the upper tibia. The patella helps reinforce the muscles responsible for knee straightening, which happens when the quadriceps contracts and pulls on the patella, which pulls on the tibia or shin.

Any activity that involves forcible straightening of the knee under pressure, for example, running up and down stairs two at a time, puts a great deal of strain on the patella.

As with the hip joint, much of the joint surface of the knee is lined with articular cartilage. Synovial fluid is also found within the joint.

There are many arteries around the knee, which bring blood from the heart to the structures of the leg. The largest is the popliteal artery, found directly behind the joint, and is a continuation of the femoral artery that has passed by the hip higher up.

Two major nerves are also found near the knee joint. These are the tibial nerve behind and the common peroneal nerve to the outside. These blood vessels and nerves are important because any trauma to the knee joint may also disrupt the blood or nerve supply to the leg.

The common peroneal nerve is particularly important because damage to this results in a drop foot deformity, that is, the patient is unable to lift the toes or ankle upwards. It can sometimes be seen after fracture, or occasionally as a complication of surgery.

As with the hip, the knee first appears as a cartilaginous structure, later ossifying. The cartilaginous femur can first be seen in the womb eight weeks after conception, the tibia appearing a little later.

The kneecap does not appear in bony form until at least the age of three years in girls, even later in boys. The knee joint as a whole ceases growth between the ages of 17 and 20 years.

In early years bones tend to be softer and more pliable than later in life. They are harder to fracture

Arteries and nerves of the knee

There are many arteries, veins and nerves around the knee, and extreme care is exercised during surgery to prevent damage.

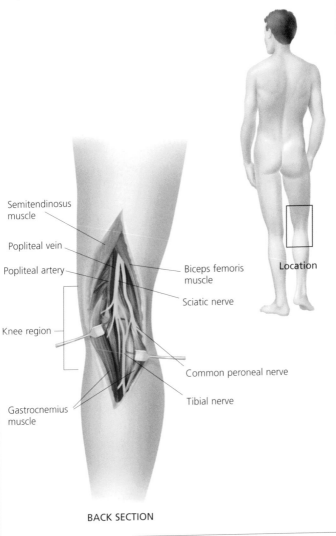

Semitendinosus muscle

Popliteal vein

Popliteal artery

Knee region

Gastrocnemius muscle

Biceps femoris muscle

Sciatic nerve

Location

Common peroneal nerve

Tibial nerve

BACK SECTION

and heal faster if they do break. Sometimes childhood injuries can lead to arthritis in future years.

There are also certain types of arthritis that are specific to children which, in turn, can lead to major surgery being required at a young age.

KEY POINTS

- The hip is a ball-and-socket joint kept within the acetabulum by strong ligaments
- The hip joint stops growing between the ages of 15 and 25
- The knee is a hinge joint, although some rotation is possible
- The knee joint stops growing between the ages of 17 and 20

Arthritis

What is arthritis?

Arthritis can take many forms. The addition of '-itis' to the end of a word usually means inflammation. Here, however, it describes a gradual damage to the joint surface.

The two most common forms of arthritis are osteoarthritis and rheumatoid arthritis, but other conditions, such as ankylosing spondylitis, systemic lupus erythematosus ('lupus') or psoriasis can cause arthritis-type damage and are known as arthropathies.

Infection can also cause problems (septic arthritis). The common feature for all forms of arthritis is a loss of the smoothness of the articular surface so that low-friction movement is replaced by irregular, gritty, high-friction agony. The joint changes can then, in turn, cause changes to the muscles and ligaments surrounding the joint.

Osteoarthritis

Osteoarthritis is often referred to as wear and tear; others may call it degeneration, but they mean the same thing. The first change that occurs in osteoarthritis is the wearing away of the cartilage which lines and protects the bony surface of a joint.

As the smooth surface of the joint disappears, so the now irregular joint surfaces creak and groan (a sound known as 'crepitus'). Small pieces of articular cartilage break off, giving rise to debris within the joint.

Sometimes these debris particles can enlarge to become loose bodies, by gathering other particles to them like snowballs rolling down a hillside. Entrapment of loose bodies may result in jamming or locking of the joint.

The gradual loss of articular cartilage is also associated with changes in the bone underneath. This bone, which used to be protected by the cartilage, starts to change shape markedly, often becoming flattened and mushroom shaped – similar to the ends of a wooden mallet that has been overused.

Various other bone changes can take place, including the formation of cysts within the bone. They are called subchondral cysts, and can occasionally reach an enormous size – five centimetres is not unknown. Also, within the osteoarthritic joint, bony protrusions start to appear at the edges, caused by new bone formation which is now deranged. These protrusions are called osteophytes and can be painful in their own right.

Eventually the articular cartilage wears down so much that the bone underneath it is exposed. Pain increases as movement against the exposed bone results in more friction. The synovial membrane which produces synovial fluid (which 'oils' the joint) also changes, becoming inflamed as a result of friction. In some cases, a synovial effusion results – this means that the joint becomes swollen and painful as too much synovial fluid is produced.

Osteoarthritis

Osteoarthritis is often referred to as wear and tear of the joints.

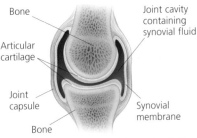

Bone

Joint cavity
containing
synovial fluid

Articular
cartilage

Joint
capsule

Synovial
membrane

Bone

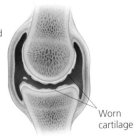

Worn
cartilage

1. A normal joint has a smooth layer of cartilage overlying healthy bone lubricated by uncontaminated synovial fluid

2. First the cartilage wears away and the smooth surface of the joint disappears

Debris in joint

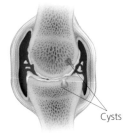

Cysts

3. Then small pieces of cartilage break off, giving rise to debris within the joint which can interrupt movement

4. Subchondral cysts may form in the bone, interfering with normal joint function and causing pain

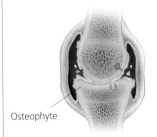

Osteophyte

5. Bony protrusions called osteophytes may appear at the edges of joints, again disrupting function and causing pain

6. Eventually the articular cartilage wears down so much that the bone is exposed. This results in further friction, which causes pain and inflames the synovial fluid

Rheumatoid arthritis

Rheumatoid arthritis is very different to osteoarthritis. Causes including abnormalities in the immune system have been suggested, but none has been proven.

It starts as an inflammation of the lining of the joint (synovium), called a synovitis. Slowly this inflammation becomes uncontrollable and results in extensive cartilage destruction.

Although rheumatoid arthritis may be confined to the hip or the knee, it frequently affects other joints in the body. The upper limbs and hands are often involved.

Rheumatoid arthritis is not classically associated with cysts in the bone or with osteophytes. However, sometimes osteoarthritis can develop in addition to rheumatoid arthritis in the same joint.

Septic arthritis

Hip and knee infections used to be very common in the west. With improved living standards such infections have become less frequent, but they are still common in the developing world.

Bacteria can enter the joint either directly, as might happen during a penetrating injury (for example, a stab wound), or through some other point in the body. For example, an infected ingrowing toenail can send bacteria to the knee or hip lying above it.

Infection in a joint can be a disaster for the articular cartilage which is extremely sensitive to the effect of bacteria. Within hours the protective surface can be damaged.

Unfortunately, articular cartilage cannot heal. Once the surface is destroyed, there is no recovering. It is for this reason that a septic arthritis is regarded as a surgical emergency.

Surgery can clean the joint, instil antibiotics and gather accurate details about the exact nature of the bacterium causing the infection, so that effective antibiotics can be given.

Other causes of arthritis

There are other conditions that can cause arthritis of the hip or knee. Bleeding disorders such as haemophilia and metabolic problems such as gout or diabetes can damage the joints.

Gout, for example, is caused by the presence of too much uric acid in the blood, often for unexplained reasons, or as a consequence of drug therapy, hypothyroidism and other hormonal imbalances, and rare metabolic diseases. Crystals of uric acid are deposited in the joints and cause excruciating pain.

Signs and symptoms of arthritis

Arthritis of the hip or knee primarily causes pain. However, it may also result in deformity or swelling. The joint may give way when weight is placed on it, or catch or creak with movement.

The pain may begin intermittently, but ultimately will become persistent. Initially it may be created only by exercise, but eventually appears at rest as well. It may sometimes be so severe as to cause night pain. Sleep becomes impossible, and the patient's general condition becomes run down as a result.

Pain felt in a hip does not always mean that the hip joint is at fault. Likewise for pain felt in the knee. 'Referred pain', that is, trouble in one part of the body causing pain in another, is something doctors frequently see. This is the result of the complex nerve supply to the various parts of the body.

Low back pain

Deformities of the hip and knee can put abnormal pressure on other joints, such as the lower vertebrae and ankles, causing further pain.

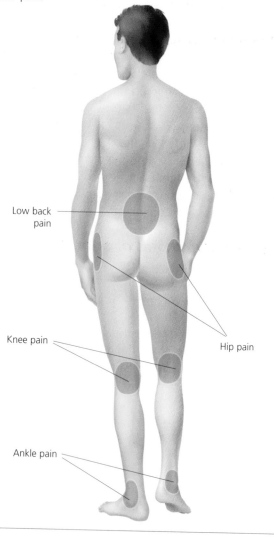

Low back pain

Hip pain

Knee pain

Ankle pain

Hip problems can sometimes be felt as pain in the knee, and back problems can occasionally be felt in the hip. Cysts in the womb, hernias, ovarian problems and many other conditions can all be felt in the hip or further down the leg. It is therefore important that any other symptoms be reported to the doctor, so that a complete and accurate picture of the problem can be built up.

As the articular cartilage becomes destroyed, so the joint deforms. The knee can become permanently bent, a deformity known as a flexion contracture. In the hip, the ball and socket also gradually bends, making it impossible for the patient to straighten the hip joint at all.

The knee may also become bowed (a varus deformity) or knock-kneed (a valgus deformity). These deformities can apply pressure on other joints such as the ankle and low back. It is thus not unusual to find that patients with arthritis of the hip or knee also have problems with back pain, or even ankle pain.

KEY POINTS

- The two most common forms of arthritis are osteoarthritis and rheumatoid arthritis

- Osteoarthritis (wear and tear) is the wearing away of the cartilage, which protects the bony surface of a joint

- Rheumatoid arthritis starts as an inflammation of the lining of the joint

- Patients with arthritis of the hip or knee can also feel pain in other areas, such as the back or even the ankle

Investigations

Seeing your doctor

Patients seeing a doctor for the first time with a
painful joint may be asked a variety of questions by the
doctor, as shown in the box. The doctor will be
particularly interested in how much handicap the
arthritis is causing. A severe handicap to one person
may be no more than an inconvenience to another.

Any decision to operate is likely to be based on the
degree of handicap that the arthritis creates. Expect to
be asked 'How much of a problem is this to you?'

The doctor may also want to know if you are stiff in
the morning, and whether you have noticed any
swelling, creaking or clicking of the joint. The doctor
may then examine the joint, feeling it for any
abnormality, and moving it to see what range of
movement it has.

Not all patients require investigation in any form (X-
rays or blood tests). In simple cases, the diagnosis is
often made solely on the patient's symptoms and the
examination. In more complex cases, the following
investigations may be done.

Blood tests

Various blood tests can be done: to check the degree of inflammation in the body; to check for infection; to look for immune system factors known as autoantibodies that are present in some forms of arthritis; to check the blood uric acid level for gout; and to check other related blood levels.

X-rays

The X-ray appearance of osteoarthritis is different from that for rheumatoid arthritis. In osteoarthritis, the osteophytes can be seen, as can bone cysts, combined with a narrowed gap between the two bone surfaces.

This narrowed gap represents the gradual erosion of the articular surfaces. Loose bodies can also be seen. For rheumatoid arthritis the situation is different. Osteophytes are not seen but there is a widespread thinning of the bone, particularly in the region of the joint, such as might be seen in a case of osteoporosis.

Blood test

A blood sample can give valuable information to assist your doctor's investigations.

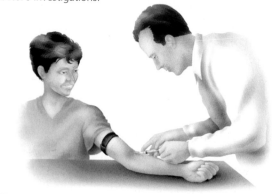

Questions that you may be asked by doctors

First visit
- How old are you?
  (*Osteoarthritis is more common in people aged over 50.*)
- What is your ethnic background?
  (*Some of the less common conditions are more common in certain ethnic groups, for example, sickle cell disease.*)
- What is your occupation?

Other questions
- Is there a family history of joint disease?
- What is your own medical history, including past injuries?
- Are you on any medication?
- How much of a problem is this to you?

Questions related to the joint pain
- When and how did the pain start?
- What has the pattern of pain been (getting worse or better)?
- Does something trigger the pain (for example, a new drug, an illness)?
- Where is the pain, where does it shoot to, what aggravates it, what relieves it, and what is the pattern of pain like during the day and night?

Frequently, the X-ray changes of rheumatoid arthritis are not severe, even though pain is intolerable. This is a reflection partly of bone and articular cartilage damage but also of the terrible agony created by the synovitis of rheumatoid arthritis. The synovial membrane cannot be seen on an X-ray.

Other investigations

Many different investigations can be undertaken to help diagnose and understand arthritis:

- Arthrography
- Magnetic resonance imaging (MRI)
- Computed tomography (CT)
- Single photon emission computed tomography (SPECT)
- Biopsy
- Aspiration
- Key hole surgery.

Arthrography

A series of X-rays of a joint after injection of a contrast medium. The injection is normally done under a local anaesthetic. Especially useful to visualise the soft tissue structures of a joint or joints.

Magnetic resonance imaging

A medical imaging technique primarily used to visualise the internal structure and function of the body. It provides detailed images of the body in any plane. MRI provides much greater contrast between the different soft tissues of the body than does computed tomography (CT).

Computed tomography

A medical imaging method used to generate a three-dimensional image of the inside of an object from a

Arthrography

A contrast medium (shows up on X-rays) is injected into the area to be studied and a series of X-rays taken to visualise the structures.

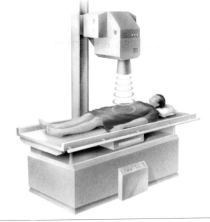

a

Magnetic resonance imaging (MRI)

Magnetic resonance imaging (MRI) can detect many subtle and small abnormalities that are invisible to CT scanning.

Computed tomography (CT)

Computed tomography (CT) fires X-rays through the brain at different angles. The X-rays are picked up by receivers and the information analysed by a computer to create a picture.

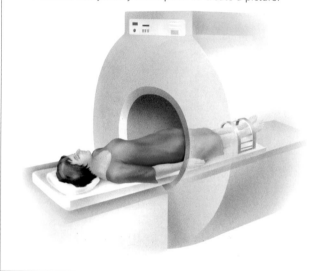

large series of two-dimensional X-ray images (slices) taken around a single axis of rotation.

Single photon emission computed tomography

A nuclear medicine imaging technique using gamma rays. The radioisotope is administered to the patient and the escaping gamma rays are recorded by a gamma camera which computes and calculates the image. To acquire SPECT images, the gamma camera is rotated around the patient. The time taken to obtain each projection is also variable, but 15 to 20 seconds is typical. This gives a total scan time of 15 to 20 minutes.

Single photon emission computed tomography (SPECT)

Isotope scanning uses a gamma camera to create a picture from gamma rays, which are emitted from the body after a radioactive isotope is swallowed or injected.

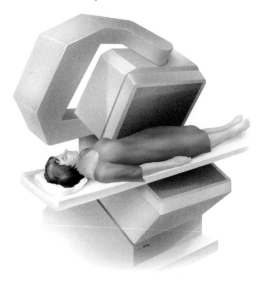

Biopsy and aspiration

Both procedures involve taking a sample from the affected joint. A biopsy involves the removal of cells or tissues for examination – usually under a microscope. Aspiration is a technique for removing some joint fluid, if swelling is present, for analysis.

Keyhole surgery (arthroscopy)

Can be performed as a method of investigation. Here small probes (4.5 millimetres in width) are inserted into the joint and specimens taken of particularly damaged

Aspiration

A syringe is used to draw fluid from the knee joint to relieve swelling and provide a sample for analysis.

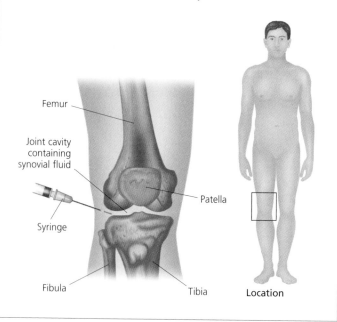

Femur

Joint cavity containing synovial fluid

Patella

Syringe

Fibula

Tibia

Location

areas if required. Hip keyhole surgery is still confined to a few specialist centres worldwide. Knee keyhole surgery is more commonly undertaken.

Case report: Margaret

Margaret, age 23 years, had experienced aching in many joints since she was a child. The aching was also associated with stiffness, somewhat worse in the morning, and she began to notice a gradually decreasing mobility.

The knuckle joints of her hands began to swell and her fingers started to deform. Her wrists began to feel

Arthroscopy

In arthroscopy, the inside of the joint is inspected with an arthroscope. Here the surgeon is operating on the knee joint.

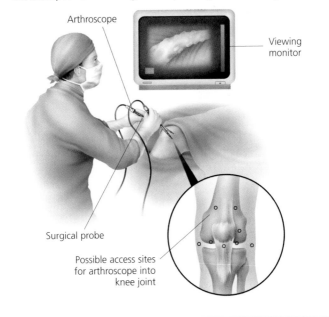

Arthroscope

Viewing monitor

Surgical probe

Possible access sites for arthroscope into knee joint

weak. Slowly, she began to experience pain in both hips and her left knee. Moreover, her left knee began to swell and become knock-kneed.

Eventually, Margaret's general practitioner advised that she should seek specialist advice, sending her to a rheumatologist. Blood tests were undertaken that identified rheumatoid arthritis, and Margaret was referred onwards to an orthopaedic surgeon. The orthopaedic surgeon performed a thorough examination, and felt that surgery had to be performed on Margaret's left knee.

Consequently, despite her young age, Margaret underwent a left total knee replacement. As a result of this her lifestyle was dramatically improved, pain has largely settled and she has been able to return to her work as an accounts clerk with a local council, an occupation that she had been unable to carry out because of debilitating pain for three years before surgery.

Case report: Tony

At the age of 24 years Tony was a top professional footballer. He had trained for many years to achieve this level, running up to 60 miles each week on the roads around his home town in preparation. Physical activity was his whole life. Now, at 58 years of age, and in secure employment as a sports adviser, his right hip was starting to get the better of him.

He had noticed increasing discomfort in both groin and knee when he walked, his walking distance now being limited to little more than 300 metres before pain stopped him. He was finding sleep difficult and a recent visit to an orthopaedic surgeon had demonstrated osteoarthritis of the right hip visible on X-ray.

The orthopaedic surgeon suggested that Tony's knee pain may be referred from his worn hip joint and had also advised him that he was too young to undergo a hip replacement, preferring to treat him initially with physiotherapy, manipulation and tablets.

Tony found that the tablets, known as anti-inflammatories, help him significantly, although they do not alleviate the pain totally. The orthopaedic surgeon has warned that a hip replacement will one day be needed.

KEY POINTS

■ Blood tests are often performed in the investigation of arthritis

■ The X-ray appearances of osteoarthritis and rheumatoid arthritis are different

■ Dye investigations (arthrography) and scans (CT, MRI) are sometimes used for investigation of arthritis

■ Keyhole surgery (arthroscopy) can also be used, and joint specimens taken for analysis

Available treatments

Is an operation the only possibility?

For arthritis of any form, surgery is usually undertaken reluctantly. It is better, and often safer, to manage the condition conservatively. Sufferers may try the effects of a range of treatments, including physiotherapy, aromatherapy, osteopathy, chiropractic, reflexology, acupuncture and diet.

There is some evidence that the popular food supplements glucosamine and chondroitin may improve the symptoms of osteoarthritis and relieve stiffness. However, despite these best efforts, conservative methods may eventually struggle to keep pace as arthritis advances. Invasive methods must therefore be considered.

Non-surgical treatments for arthritis

- Physiotherapy: treatment using physical methods rather than drugs and surgery
- Aromatherapy: use of aromatic plant extracts and essential oils
- Osteopathy: manipulation and massage of the skeleton and musculature
- Chiropractic: manipulative treatment of mechanical disorders of the joints
- Reflexology: a system of massage through reflex points on the feet, hands and head
- Acupuncture: treatment by pricking the skin or tissues with needles

Injections into the joint

The simplest invasive method is an injection, where a mixture of local anaesthetic and steroid preparation is inserted into the painful joint. The local anaesthetic has a temporary pain-relieving effect, but the steroid may be long-lasting. Its task is to reduce the inflammation associated with arthritis.

Steroids are a large group of drugs with varying actions; they are chemically related, and include contraceptive hormones, medication used by people with asthma, and even drugs used illegally by athletes and those used by body-builders.

More recently, a technique known as viscosupplementation has appeared. A single injection, or a series of injections, of a material called hyaluronic acid is given into an arthritic joint. The aim is to lubricate the joint and help with pain relief. Early results are promising.

Steroid and anaesthetic injections

An injection of local anaesthetic and steroid into the painful joint is often a very effective treatment.

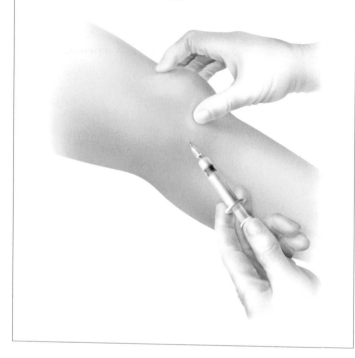

Surgical treatments for arthritis

Despite injection, arthritis can still progress, with surgery being the final solution. Over many centuries surgeons have designed a number of operations to deal with the ravages of arthritis. The following operations can be performed under either general or local anaesthetic. A combination of the two is sometimes also used. A reasonable level of health is required in order to undergo such surgery, although in case of doubt an anaesthetist is often asked to advise beforehand.

Osteotomy

Osteotomy means cutting through bone. At one time it was widely performed for arthritis of the hip and knee. It aims to create a surgical fracture so that the hip or knee may be realigned, thus causing the stresses of walking to pass through the joint in a different manner.

For example, a bow leg can be osteotomised to make it straighter. When bowed, the forces of walking pass through the inner aspect of the knee, causing it to wear faster. With the knee properly aligned, the forces pass through the centre of the knee so that both sides of the joint take a fair share of the weight.

Osteotomy – bone realignment

An osteotomy creates a surgical fracture so the hip or knee may be realigned when the bone is rejoined.

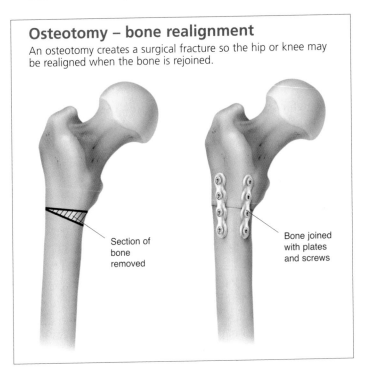

Section of bone removed

Bone joined with plates and screws

The same logic can apply to the hip, osteotomy being performed just below the level of the greater trochanter.

Osteotomies are big procedures and successful only in certain, selected groups of patients. They are more successful for individuals who, before the operation, have a good range of motion of the diseased joint. The worse the range of motion, the less likely it is that osteotomy will improve matters.

Osteotomy can also alter the length of a patient's leg, leaving it either shorter or longer than the other side after surgery. The procedure can take about 90 minutes to perform.

Case report: John

John was a 42-year-old soldier. Ten years previously he had sustained a dislocation of his right hip in a bad parachuting accident. The hip had been put back into joint at the time, but this did not protect him from a gradual development of osteoarthritis.

As he was still relatively young, his orthopaedic surgeon advised against joint replacement, because such operations only last a certain number of years – 10 years maximum would be a reasonable estimate as in John's case.

Instead, particularly as his range of hip movement was good, an osteotomy was advised. A cut was made across the bone just below the greater trochanter and the femur twisted slightly to alter the stresses through the hip joint.

This improved John's pain dramatically. The osteotomy site was held together by plates and screws. John was on crutches for three months after surgery, noticing that one leg was very slightly shorter after the operation than it had been before.

This did not bother him as a small heel raise was provided once he was allowed to walk free of crutch support. John was delighted with the result, though he realises that a hip replacement will one day be required.

Arthroscopy

Arthroscopy, or keyhole surgery, is now widely performed. More than a million such operations are performed worldwide each year. It is uncommon to use arthroscopy for the hip, but it is widely used on the knee.

The principle is to insert a small probe, usually 4.5 millimetres (mm) in diameter, into the joint under general or local anaesthetic. This allows an excellent view of all structures within the area and a very accurate assessment of the progress of the condition.

The procedure can be used for all forms of arthritis and is usually quick – 45 minutes would be the norm. With the keyhole instrument (arthroscope) inserted into the joint, operating instruments may be inserted via other small incisions. It is possible to remove loose bodies, clean joint surfaces, tidy up cartilages and trim ligaments easily with an arthroscope.

However, what an arthroscope cannot do is eliminate arthritis. The effects on a patient's symptoms are variable. Some patients claim dramatic pain relief, whereas others can say that their discomfort is worse.

The use of the arthroscope in the management of arthritis must therefore be approached with caution. As its complication rate is low (one case of infection in 2,000 operations, for example), it is commonly used to buy time for a joint before more major surgery is considered. It is particularly useful in younger individuals who are still very active and for whom more major surgery such as joint replacement would be

Arthroscopy

Arthroscopy, or keyhole surgery, involves insertion of a small viewing probe into the joint under local anaesthetic. This gives a good view of the inside of the structure and allows minor surgical procedures on the inside of the joint to be undertaken simultaneously and without wide excision.

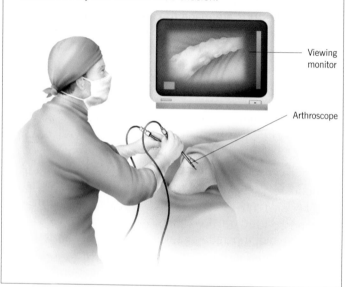

Viewing
monitor

Arthroscope

unwise. A major area of expansion in the field of hip arthroscopic surgery is in the treatment of a condition called 'impingement', when the front of the upper part of the femur catches on the front of the hip socket. This can lead to soft tissue tears and osteoarthritis. Hip arthroscopic surgeons attempt to remove the impinging area, usually as a day-case procedure.

Transplantation

Transplantation is not only confined to the heart, liver and lungs. Joints can be transplanted and have been so for many years. Bone transplantation even appears in the Bible! If arthritic damage to a joint surface is fairly localised, it is possible to remove the trouble and to insert transplanted tissue instead.

This tissue is usually taken from a dead donor. Stringent efforts are made to keep the articular cartilage cells alive before implantation into a recipient. Transplanted tissue may also be taken from animals, although this is rare.

Sometimes, an arthritis patient may undergo two operations: the first removes articular cartilage cells from one part of the body, the second re-implants them into the arthritic area. In the intervening period the cartilage cells are sent to a laboratory where they are cultured to increase their number. This procedure is called chondrocyte culture and takes approximately one hour to perform. The long-term result of procedures such as chondrocyte culture are still unknown.

However, there is currently widespread research worldwide into attempts to replace the cartilage surface before it becomes fully osteoarthritic to establish its efficacy. It is likely that there will be major changes in this area within the next 10 years.

Carbon fibre and other synthetic materials

If arthritis affects all parts of a joint, then the only suitable surgical treatment is for the whole joint area to be operated on. However, in its early stages, arthritis can affect just one area of the joint. If so, carbon fibre can be implanted, the damaged area being cut away and carbon fibre implanted in its place.

Carbon fibre comes in various forms, but small cylindrical pegs are particularly common. The object of the carbon fibre is to provide a scaffold along which patients can grow their own bone and cartilage-type tissue. The growth process can take several months and can encourage the damaged area to recover. Ceramics, metals and plastics have also been used.

The results are unpredictable, with articular cartilage only rarely reforming reliably. Such so-called resurfacing procedures are not widely performed as a result of their variable results. They are, however, particularly applicable to the younger patient with localised areas of cartilage damage rather than generalised disease in the joint.

Arthrodesis

Arthrodesis means fusion of a joint. Patients with arthritis experience pain caused by joint movement. The more it is moved, the worse the discomfort. Consequently, fusing the joint surgically is one way of eliminating pain altogether.

The operation takes about 90 minutes to perform. However, by performing an arthrodesis, greater strain is taken up by the joints either side of the fused one. For example, with a knee fusion the hip and ankle take greater strain. With a hip fusion, the knee and back take greater strain.

The advantage of an arthrodesis is that it does not involve the implantation of mobile joint replacement parts. As a result there is very little to go wrong. However, walking can be impaired because it is not possible to walk with a normal gait after either a hip or a knee fusion. The operated leg is sometimes shorter than its untouched partner but the results are at least permanent.

If necessary an arthrodesed joint can be converted to a joint replacement, but the results of these so-called

Arthrodesis

Arthrodesis means fusion of a joint to eliminate joint pain.

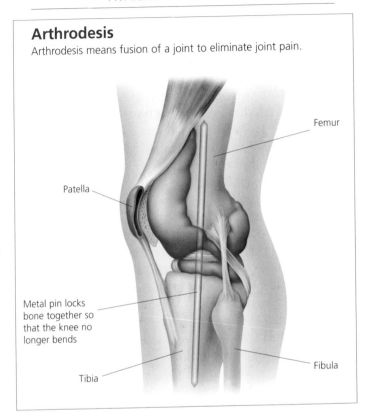

Femur

Patella

Metal pin locks
bone together so
that the knee no
longer bends

Tibia

Fibula

'conversion' operations are not always as good as
replacement of a previously unoperated joint.

Case report: Joyce

Joyce was a 22-year-old woman who had been
involved in a road traffic accident eight years previously.
The accident had caused a fracture of her tibial
plateau. Despite capable and accurate reconstruction
by emergency orthopaedic teams, the knee joint
subsequently developed arthritis. Pain gradually

worsened until orthopaedic surgeons advised that she should have an arthrodesis.

Naturally, Joyce was wary of the prospect of having her knee fused, but pain was dominating every aspect of her life. She understood that a joint replacement would not last forever. Although there was no limit to the number of times it could be redone, each successive operation would not last as long as the one preceding it. Eventually, the knee would become inoperable and amputation might be required.

Joyce was naturally very worried about this. Osteotomy was also unsuitable because the fracture had deformed her upper tibia so much that surgery would have been technically very difficult, with a real risk of damage to her major blood vessels and nerves.

Consequently, Joyce accepted the idea of an arthrodesis. Her knee is now fused in a straight position and she finds life has opened up for her despite this apparent handicap. Her knee is totally pain free, she is able to drive a specially adapted car and is now at work as the manager of a charity shop.

To date she has not experienced any discomfort in her hip or ankle, although has been warned that this may occur in years to come. She knows this is at least 20 years away.

Débridement

Débridement is a surgical term for cleaning of an area. Arthritis is associated with the development of loose bodies, debris and osteophytes. These can be locally tender, or they can cause a joint to jam and give way. Consequently, to remove them is sometimes beneficial.

Such a débridement operation does not eliminate arthritis entirely, but it may delay the day when more significant surgery is required. It can sometimes be performed arthroscopically, although it is frequently undertaken as an open operation, when a large surgical incision is performed. This allows good access to all nooks and crannies of the joint so that a wide cleaning procedure may then be undertaken.

Results are variable, with full pain relief unlikely. However, débridement can buy time for the younger patient before major surgery is required or can be helpful for the older patient who is not fit enough for a long anaesthetic. The procedure itself can take as little as 30 to 45 minutes to perform.

Joint replacement

Replacement of the hip or knee joints, although a major undertaking, represents one of the most major advances in surgery of recent times. The quality-of-life improvement is nearly equivalent to that seen after heart bypass surgery, patients noticing an enormous improvement in mobility and a dramatic decline in pain levels. Joint replacements take up to two hours to perform, and do not always last forever.

Theoretically, they can be replaced any number of times. However, each successive operation is usually less successful than the previous one.

The author's personal record is 19 total hip replacements in one patient – although he did not do the previous 18! As a result, younger patients are offered such surgery with reluctance.

The principle of a joint replacement is to remove the arthritic area and to replace it with artificial or synthetic materials. The operation will be considered in more detail in subsequent chapters.

Resurfacing

For the younger patient with an osteoarthritic hip, the operation of resurfacing has appeared. This involves placing a metal cap over the hip ball and a metal liner in the socket.

The attraction is that it removes less bone from a patient than a full hip replacement, so that there is more bone available for the surgeon when a hip replacement is eventually required.

Resurfacing is now becoming more widely performed, results showing that 95 per cent or more of hip resurfacings are still working well at least eight years after surgery. The ball of a resurfacing has a wider diameter than that of a total hip replacement, so the chances of dislocation of a resurfacing after surgery are dramatically reduced. However, although resurfacing is clearly an attractive operation, longer-term results are still awaited.

Some worries have recently begun to emerge about the procedure. For example, the metal ball and the metal liner from which a resurfacing is made can cause the levels of metal in the blood to rise. It is not known whether this is of long-term consequence to the patient.

In addition, there is a higher chance of fracturing the upper part of the femur (femoral neck) after resurfacing surgery, and some patients experience groin pain, often thought to be caused by the irritation of a muscle known as iliopsoas on the front of the resurfacing components.

Should a resurfacing fail then the principle is that it can be converted to a total hip replacement. However, how a total hip replacement will fare after a resurfacing has been performed is, as yet, unknown. In general, it appears that resurfacing is a good operation but it

Hip resurfacing

Hip resurfacing involves placing a metal cap over the hip ball and a metal liner in the socket.

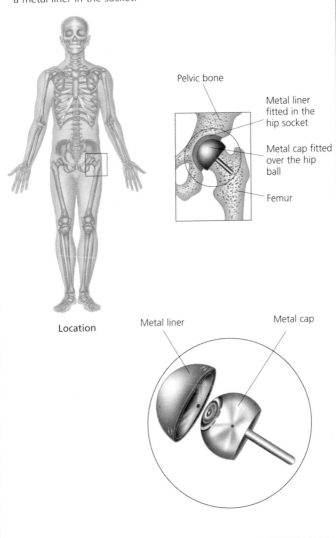

Location

Pelvic bone

Metal liner fitted in the hip socket

Metal cap fitted over the hip ball

Femur

Metal liner

Metal cap

should still be approached with caution until longer-term results are available.

Case report: Mark

Mark had once been an internationally recognised motorcycle racer. Unfortunately his career had come to a rapid end when he dislocated his hip in a near-fatal accident. He was only 28 years old at the time.

By the time he was aged 30 years, the hip had become rapidly osteoarthritic and the pain was intolerable. He was unable to sleep at night, medication did not help him and he found that he was always in a bad mood. He argued with everybody. His surgeon recommended that he should receive a hip resurfacing. Mark readily agreed.

The operation went well and Mark was in hospital for only four days. Within six weeks of surgery he had returned to gentle physical activity and now, three years later, he is back to his motorcycle racing, completely pain free. He has also performed a tandem free-fall parachute descent for a local charity. He has not dared tell his surgeon!

Case report: Robert

Robert was a 48-year-old accountant who had once represented his country as a marathon runner. However, he had a strong family history of hip arthritis and it was perhaps no surprise to him that his own right hip had begun to become a problem in his late 30s.

It had started to ruin his quality of life. All his sporting activities had been curtailed and night pain was a significant issue. His orthopaedic surgeon identified severe osteoarthritis of the hip and recommended that Robert undergo a hip resurfacing operation.

The surgeon explained that this involved placing a metal cap on the femoral head (ball of hip joint) and a metal liner in the socket, although the long-term results of the operation were still not known. However, the resurfacing involved less bone being removed from Robert's hip at surgery and there was always the alternative of conversion to a total hip replacement if the resurfacing failed.

Robert was delighted to accept this suggestion, underwent a successful hip resurfacing and returned to sport four months later. However, he did accept his surgeon's recommendation that marathon running should be avoided after a hip resurfacing and that mountain biking would be a better alternative.

KEY POINTS

■ For arthritis of any form, surgery is usually undertaken reluctantly because it is often safer to manage the condition conservatively

■ Osteotomy, the division of a bone and realignment, is sometimes used for arthritis

■ Arthroscopy (keyhole surgery) is widely used in arthritis, although not always successfully

■ Joint replacement is widely used, although caution is needed in young patients

■ Resurfacing is now increasingly performed, although longer-term results of the operation are still awaited

Hip replacement

Why replace the hip?

The hip is replaced for three reasons:

1 Pain
2 Deformity
3 Protection of other joints.

Pain from joint damage is often the overriding factor when deciding to replace the hip.

Pain may be unremitting, dominating every aspect of life and making physical activity almost impossible. Sometimes the hip can be deformed, so that the body is bent forwards at the hip, or the ball can sink deeply into the socket (a condition known as 'protrusio').

The presence of a stiff hip can also occasionally overload the lower back.

Certain inflammatory conditions can affect both the low back and the hips. Ankylosing spondylitis is an example. Here the spine is primarily affected, but the hips can also be extensively involved. Replacement of the hips can therefore be protective of the spine.

History of hip replacement

Hip replacement is not new. The first was performed in 1891 by a Dr Gluck. Then, in 1926, Professor Hey Groves described the use of an ivory hip replacement.

Designs developed thereafter, some with the use of a Perspex-like material, until the late 1950s when the widely used metal ball and plastic socket was introduced. Now, most hip replacements are of this design.

The two parts of a hip replacement are the femoral component (artificial upper thigh bone) and the acetabular component (artificial hip socket). It is normal for the femoral component to be made of metal (for example, stainless steel or titanium) and the acetabular component to be made of polyethylene. Both components are traditionally cemented into their respective bones with a cement called polymethyl-methacrylate (PMMA).

Cementless components are specially designed in order to encourage bone to grow into them, so that the artificial hip replacement becomes tightly secured to the patient. Some of the artificial components are roughened with tiny beads, a layer called porous coating.

Other cementless components are coated in a material called hydroxyapatite, which encourages bone to grow into it remarkably quickly. The end result can be a secure component without the use of cement at all.

Not all surgeons are happy with the use of cement because it can sometimes create problems if the hip needs to be revised. Artificial hips can therefore sometimes be cemented, and sometimes cementless.

Cement has been perceived by some as being difficult to remove if revision surgery is ever needed.

Hip replacement

The two parts of a hip replacement are the femoral component (artificial upper thigh bone) and the acetabular component (artificial hip socket).

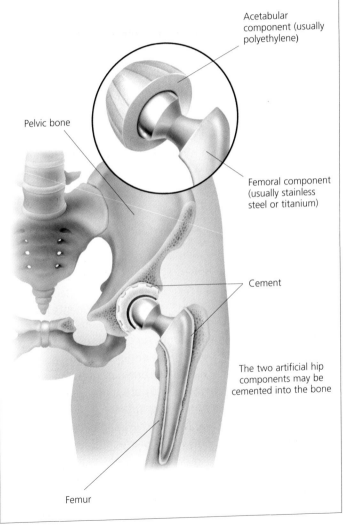

Acetabular component (usually polyethylene)

Pelvic bone

Femoral component (usually stainless steel or titanium)

Cement

The two artificial hip components may be cemented into the bone

Femur

Cement versus cementless

The two components of an artificial hip are traditionally cemented into their respective bones. A cementless fixing requires the bone to grow and fuse with the artificial components.

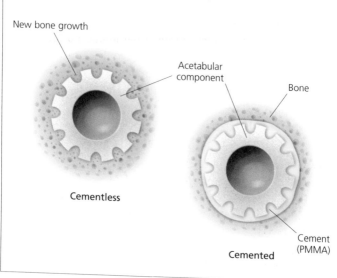

New bone growth

Acetabular component

Bone

Cementless

Cement (PMMA)

Cemented

This can be true, although instruments now exist to remove cement more easily: high-speed cutters, special light sources, even ultrasound. As a result of the perceived difficulties of cement removal, many younger patients who require a joint replacement are offered cementless replacements as they are more likely eventually to need a revision operation.

Occasionally it is possible for the femoral component to be cemented and the acetabular component to be cementless. This is because some surgeons believe that cemented acetabular components are a source of weakness in a hip replacement and are best avoided. There is still much debate in orthopaedic circles about this. This mixture of fixations gives rise to the term 'hybrid' hip replacement.

One way in which hip replacements fail is as a result of the production of small polyethylene particles (from the acetabular component), or wear debris. This debris can result in a low-grade inflammation affecting the bone of either the femur or acetabulum, or both. This leads to bone loss, or osteolysis.

To minimise osteolysis it has been suggested that the metal-on-plastic articulation has too high a friction and other materials have been investigated.

A ceramic-on-plastic articulation has been tried, and also ceramic on ceramic, whereas special plastic materials have been developed to increase their strength and reduce friction still further.

Metal-on-metal articulations have also been considered, the femoral component having a metal ball and the acetabulum having no plastic in it whatsoever, being made entirely of metal. This combination can also be used for some of the modern, so-called 'resurfacing' operations.

Despite the many different designs, a metal ball-and-plastic socket are still the most common components used today.

Preparing for the operation

Having a hip replacement involves major surgery, and every patient can aid their recovery by being as prepared for the consequences as possible.

The best way to make the operation as easy as possible for the surgeon and the anaesthetist is to maintain a high degree of general fitness before the operation, even with a painful hip. The items in the box on page 54 should be followed.

How you can help your recovery from an operation

- Stopping smoking: smokers are more liable to have breathing complications while they are under anaesthetic, and also more prone to chest infection after the operation. This can prolong the period of bed rest and delay a patient getting back on their feet.

- Losing weight: an overweight patient is harder to operate on than a slim one. The hip is covered with more flesh, so more flesh needs to be cut to expose the hip properly, which leads to more bleeding. It is also physically more difficult (heavier work) for the surgeons who have to manipulate the leg during surgery. Very overweight patients are also more liable to have breathing difficulties under anaesthesia. Patients should lose whatever weight they can as every kilogram helps. Less weight will also put less strain on the replacement.

- Drugs: prescription drugs for heart or blood pressure should be taken regularly so that the patient is as fit for the operation as possible.

- Exercise: patients should try to do whatever exercise they can manage, as the fitter they are the easier it will be to get back on their feet. The physiotherapist at the hospital can recommend exercises to strengthen specific parts of the body – for instance, the arms, so that they can support the body better after the operation.

A few changes to your home may be necessary in preparation for your return after the operation. As part of hospital assessment, patients are frequently asked to describe the facilities that they have in their homes. This is to ensure that necessary appliances are available when they return after surgery.

For example, chairs should not be too low, baths should be fitted with hand rails, banisters should be available for stairs, and beds neither too soft nor too low (see later section on 'When can I …?' for details). This is the territory of the occupational therapist who can both recommend and supply much of the needed equipment (see 'Useful addresses', page 121).

On admission to hospital

The operation of hip replacement may be performed under general or local anaesthetic, or sometimes a combination of the two.

As with other major surgery, the patient has to be assessed before the operation to make sure that they are fit for the operation. Usually a full medical history will be taken, and various tests performed. These could include those in the box on page 56.

Admission is either on the day of surgery or the day before. Blood thinning drugs (anticoagulants) may be given to reduce the chance of blood clots forming in the calf veins, a complication with which major surgery can be associated, known as deep vein thrombosis (DVT).

These clots are more easily formed because during and after the operation the patient is bed-bound for some time, and not moving the legs as much as possible. Blood flow in the legs slows as a result, and can slow down to the extent that clots are formed.

Tests before the operation

Before the operation you will be assessed to ensure you are suitable for an operation. Tests may include:

- Blood tests to check for anaemia, and to make sure that the blood electrolytes or salts are at a normal level. Blood will also be taken for blood grouping and supplies ordered in case you need a transfusion after the operation. Some patients elect to donate their own blood for later transfusion, a process called autologous transfusion.

- Urine is also tested because it is essential that no evidence of a urinary tract infection is present at the time of surgery. If this happens, there is a small chance that the hip replacement can also become infected.

- X-rays of the chest to check that there is no chest infection – which can lead to breathing difficulties during and after the operation – and to check that the heart outline is normal and the heart can withstand the operation.

- X-rays of the hip to guide the surgeons. Occasionally a CT scan may be performed.

- An ECG or electrocardiogram – a heart tracing to ensure the heart is functioning normally.

(The effect is similar to taking a long haul flight – DVTs are more common after air travel.)

Premedication may also be given in order to relax the patient and make the general anaesthetic a smoother experience. Antibiotics are usually given at the time of operation to reduce the chance of infection afterwards.

Not all hip replacements are performed using general anaesthesia. Many are undertaken using either local anaesthesia alone, or a combination of general and local anaesthesia. In some countries it is more common to undergo a hip replacement using local rather than general anaesthesia.

The operation

The operation involves the removal of the arthritic hip joint and the insertion of artificial components. It can be performed with the patient lying either flat on the back or on the side, and the incision can be anything from 7 to 35 centimetres long.

Generally speaking, the more fat there is around the joint, the longer the incision has to be, as the joint is more hidden. Skin incisions that are less than 10 centimetres long are sometimes called 'minimal incisions'.

The operation of minimal incision hip replacement is becoming very popular with both patients and surgeons, although the amount of bone that is removed is the same, whatever the size of the skin incision.

Some surgeons make two small incisions rather than one larger incision. The hope is that a smaller skin incision will mean that patients can go home earlier after surgery, but the technique is still under investigation and its detailed results are still unknown.

The surgeon divides the skin, and the tissues (including muscles and ligaments) beneath it, in order to expose the hip joint.

The hip is then dislocated, and the femoral head is removed with a special saw. Once the femoral head has been removed, the acetabulum is revealed. The

The hip replacement operation

1. The surgeon divides the skin and the tissues beneath it to expose the hip joint

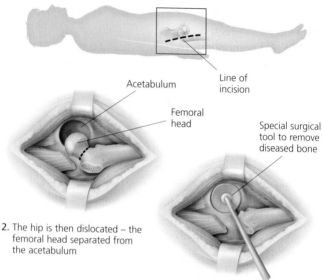

Acetabulum

Line of incision

Femoral head

Special surgical tool to remove diseased bone

2. The hip is then dislocated – the femoral head separated from the acetabulum

3. The femoral head is removed revealing the acetabulum. The arthritic bone is then all extracted with special surgical tools

Acetabular component

Femoral component

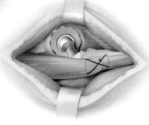

4. The first artificial item to be inserted is the acetabular component. The artificial femoral component is then inserted

5. Once both components are fixed securely, the hip is then put back in the joint, and the wound closed by stitches or clips

arthritic bone within it is then extracted with special surgical tools called reamers. It is important that all diseased bone is removed, leaving healthy bone behind. Healthy bone accepts a hip replacement much better than diseased bone.

The first component to be inserted is the acetabular component. Once this is fixed into the socket the femoral component is inserted. Some surgeons use computerised assistance to ensure proper alignment of the components whereas others use special guides known as 'jigs' to do this during the operation.

Once both components are fixed securely, the hip is then put back into the joint, a process known as reduction, and the various layers of muscle and skin are stitched or clipped together again.

The new joint is held in place by the muscle surrounding it, which will strengthen as the wound heals. Small plastic drains may be left in place in order to mop up the last few drops of blood from the muscle and wound after surgery.

However hard a surgeon tries, it is not possible to stop all the bleeding at the time of the operation. Nature does the rest within a short period of the operation. About 30 per cent of patients will require blood transfusion after a hip replacement operation.

After the operation

Gradual rehabilitation after hip replacement is essential. It is normal for patients to stay in bed for one or two days after the procedure, although there is now an increasing trend for patients to be mobilised more rapidly than was the case in earlier years.

It is now not unknown for patients to be asked to get out of bed and walk only a few hours after their operation. In many orthopaedic units it is traditional for a triangular pillow to be placed between the legs, apex up. This is referred to as an abduction wedge, keeping the legs apart and thereby maintaining hip stability.

Particularly in the early days after surgery, it is possible for the ball to slip out of the socket, a complication known as dislocation (see 'Complications' pages 62–7). Some surgeons have now abandoned the use of an abduction wedge and claim that it has made no difference to their rate of postoperative dislocation.

Much of the postoperative rehabilitation associated with replacement is aimed at reducing the chances of dislocation. This is largely the task of the physiotherapist who will move the hip joint and teach the patient

Abduction wedge

An abduction wedge keeps the legs apart, maintaining hip stability in the early stages of recovery. It is not always used after surgery.

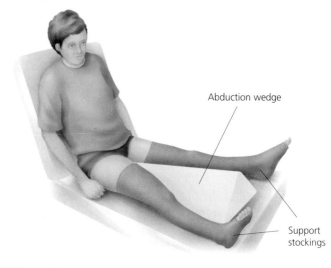

Abduction wedge

Support stockings

those movements that are safe to perform after replacement surgery.

Exercising the leg within these limits can also help prevent blood clots forming, and patients may also be given special support stockings to help prevent the formation of a blood clot (DVT) in the leg veins.

For the first few days after the procedure, it is likely that the patient will walk supported by a walking frame. This will rapidly be replaced by crutches, and then by walking stick support. However, it is sometimes possible that a patient will be asked to remain non-weight-bearing for between six weeks and three months after the procedure.

This is particularly so if a complex bone grafting procedure has been performed at the time of hip replacement, or with the use of certain cementless designs. This is to allow time for the patient's bone to grow into, and around, the artificial hip, to ensure security of the implanted components.

Support stockings

Support stockings are worn for a few days after the operation to reduce the risk of blood clots forming.

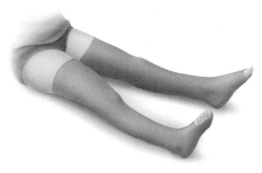

Being asked to non-weight-bear after surgery does not mean that something has gone wrong. It may simply be the wisest way of ensuring a long-lasting hip replacement.

The timing of discharge from hospital depends on many factors and can be very different from hospital to hospital. Some will discharge patients as early as the day after surgery whereas others may keep their hip replacement patients in hospital for seven to ten days, sometimes longer.

Whenever a patient is discharged home, care and caution should be taken for at least six weeks. Stitches are removed at about ten days but clips, if used to close the skin wound, are sometimes removed earlier.

Occasionally, stitches can be used that dissolve under the skin, sometimes used with a type of skin glue, so that there is no need for formal stitch removal after surgery.

Complications

It is naturally important that a patient is not worse after surgery than before. Although complications are uncommon, they do exist. It is therefore essential to make a fully informed decision before proceeding with the operation.

Complications are many and varied. Most are minor, associated with surgery in general rather than being specific to hip replacement. For the older patient, particularly those aged more than 80 years, the chances of complications increase. If a hip replacement has to be redone, an operation known as revision, there is a still higher rate of complications.

Complications may occur during surgery, or after it. They can be divided into those that occur as a result of any major surgery (general complications) and those that are particular to hip replacements (specific complications).

General complications
Infection (less than one per cent)
This will often be treated with strong antibiotics and rest, although occasionally repeat (revision) surgery is required.

Haematoma (or large bruise) formation at the wound
Occasionally the blood collected in the bruise has to be removed by opening the wound again.

Wound dehiscence
This means that the wound splits open again and has to be restitched.

Entrapped drain (very rare)
Occasionally the small plastic drain becomes stuck and a further operation is required to remove it.

Urinary complications (up to 35 per cent)
It is quite common for patients to have difficulty passing urine after surgery. This is often the result of the difficulty experienced by some in passing urine while lying down. It can occasionally be a problem when there have been previous symptoms of urinary difficulty, such as can be found with an enlarged prostate gland. For this reason a small tube (catheter) can be passed into the bladder to assist urination for a few days.

Gastrointestinal complications (one per cent)
These can sometimes be the result of anaesthetic,

blood chemical imbalance, or even the magnitude of the operation. The intestines stop working for a few days, known as an 'ileus'. This is often treated by what surgeons call 'drip and suck'. A fine plastic tube is passed through the mouth into the stomach while fluid is given through an intravenous infusion rather than by mouth. As soon as the intestines recover their function the drip-and-suck treatment is discontinued.

Cardiovascular complications (up to 60 per cent)

Surgical stress can sometimes be so great that a heart attack can occur, although this happens in less than half a per cent of patients. Occasionally a blood clot can form on the brain to give rise to a stroke.

Deep vein thrombosis (DVT) and pulmonary embolism (PE)

A DVT (deep vein thrombosis) is a blood clot that forms, usually in one of the deep veins in the leg. One of the most common situations in which a DVT can form is during an operation, especially during hip and knee surgery. This is because the blood flow through the legs is sluggish when a patient is immobile and so the blood is more likely to clot.

Occasionally part of the blood clot breaks off and travels in the blood to the lungs. This is called a pulmonary embolus (PE) and in some cases can be fatal. Because of these risks patients may be given blood thinning drugs (anticoagulants) and other measures such as special support stockings to wear to help prevent a blood clot forming.

Breathing complications

These occur mainly as a result of the anaesthetic and

the bedrest. Patients with previous chest or heart problems may be more prone to this.

Death (about one per cent)
This can be for a variety of reasons – usually related to breathing or heart complications that develop during the operation.

Specific complications
Dislocation (up to five per cent and two per cent for resurfacing)
Here, the ball slips out of the socket. A further anaesthetic is usually required to relocate it, followed either by a period of bedrest or by a period spent in a supporting hip brace. A further, open operation is only rarely needed.

Fracture (less than one per cent for initial replacement; about three per cent for revision hip replacement; almost unheard of for hip resurfacing)
This usually occurs during the operation as a result of the high stresses to which bone is subjected at surgery. Occasionally a fracture is not identified during the operation, but is seen on the first X-ray taken after the operation. If seen during the operation, the surgeon will often deal with the matter directly, perhaps surrounding the bone with strengthening wire, or inserting a screw and plates. If seen after surgery there may be a need for a further operation or, perhaps, extended bedrest to allow the fracture to unite naturally.

Nerve damage during surgery (maximum 3.5 per cent)
With nerves passing so close to the hip joint it is not

surprising that they are occasionally damaged. Most recover naturally, over a lengthy period (perhaps one to two years). A few do not recover, which can cause mobility problems for the patient.

Persistent pain over the greater trochanter (up to 17 per cent)

Known as 'trochanteric bursitis', this is a localised pain over the outer part of the hip. It is of no functional significance, but can sometimes be distressing for the patient. It does not always settle, even with time.

Prosthetic displacement

In this the artificial hip changes position within the joint. This is rare, but occasionally the artificial components can subside further into the bone. A femoral component, for example, can slip downwards within the femur whereas an acetabular component can protrude into the socket further. It is normally a reflection of weakness of the patient's supporting bone and may occasionally require reoperation.

Leg length inequality (six per cent)

One of the most common complications of hip replacement surgery is the creation of leg length inequality. It is more usual for the operated side to end up longer; there is an occasional need for a shoe raise on the other leg to compensate for this.

Nerve damage arising after the operation (less than one per cent)

Bleeding can continue after surgery, although usually only for a short time. However, blood can accumulate around a nerve and cause damage. The effect can be the same as if the nerve was directly damaged at surgery.

Blood vessel complications (0.4 per cent for initial replacement; less than one per cent for revision replacement)

As with nerves, some major blood vessels pass close by the hip joint. They, too, can be damaged at surgery.

Groin pain (up to five percent)

This appears to be more common after hip resurfacing than hip replacement and is probably caused by irritation of soft tissues on the artificial hip components; this applies particularly to a muscle known as iliopsoas. There is sometimes a need for further surgery to try to alleviate this.

Raised blood metal levels

Some hip replacements, and most resurfacings, use a metal ball and a metal liner, both made of cobalt–chrome alloy. This can result in raised cobalt and chromium levels in the bloodstream after surgery. The metal levels rise quite sharply shortly after surgery but decline over about two years, although they do not always return to normal levels. It is not known if these raised metal levels are detrimental to the patient. It appears unlikely, but much research is currently being carried out to establish this.

Results
Total hip replacement results

Many factors determine the lifespan of a total hip replacement. The age of the patient is important.

The younger the patient, the shorter the hip replacement is likely to last.

A study performed in the early 1980s looked at over 100 patients under the age of 45 years. After four and a half years only 76 per cent of their hip replacements were performing satisfactorily.

It is for this reason that great caution is taken when advising younger patients to undergo hip replacement surgery. For these patients a resurfacing procedure may be recommended.

After the age of 65 years, results improve. About 90 per cent of hips will last at least 12 years, particularly if of the fully cemented design.

Cementless hip replacements are good, but not all can compete with the results for cemented designs. They are not always easier to revise. The author, who is well used to revisions, has failed with two revision cases in the last 10 years. Both of these were cementless components that he was unable to remove.

Hip resurfacing results

Hip resurfacing, recently widely reported, still does not have sufficiently long-term results available to allow it to be compared with a full hip replacement.

The way in which the hip replacement is performed is also vital. To give an example, in one particular design the failure rate was reported as between one per cent and 24 per cent, depending on where the operation was performed – the surgeon's experience is vital. Ask your surgeon what their experience is of the operation, and what their complication and failure rates are.

Failure is sometimes the result of certain aspects of the patient, however. For instance, if the patient is overweight it makes surgery difficult. The wound is so much deeper and the joint harder to get access to, and generally there is also more bleeding in the wound.

The failure rate of revision replacements (when the operation is redone) is also very significant. Revisions of revisions, now not unknown, can give a failure rate as high as 60 per cent. Consequently, it is essential that a hip replacement is performed as well as possible on the first occasion.

Case report: Martin

Martin was a 61-year-old painter and decorator. He had suffered from osteoarthritis of his right hip for many years and had struggled on with his job for some time. Eventually he could continue no longer and followed the suggestion of his local orthopaedic surgeon that the hip should be replaced.

Martin received a cemented hip replacement. Surgery went well and he was discharged from hospital on the seventh postoperative day. Over the next six weeks he mobilised gradually and steadily, abandoning the use of crutches at the six-week point.

By three months he was walking with the aid of one walking stick, held in his left hand. He was told it was important that the stick should be held in the hand opposite the side of the replacement. Right hip, left hand – left hip, right hand.

Martin noticed an immediate relief of pain after surgery. There was natural surgical pain, but this settled within four or five days. His arthritis pain disappeared instantly. Three months after the procedure he asked his surgeon if he could return to work.

The surgeon agreed that he could do so, but that his duties would have to be modified slightly to ensure that he did not bend too low, lift too much heavy weight, and could take life easy when he wished. Martin is delighted with the result of his hip replacement.

Case report: Janet

Janet was a 72-year-old woman, previously fit and well, who fractured her left hip. The event was completely unexpected, happening when she stumbled over a pavement while shopping locally. She was taken into hospital and given a total hip replacement, of a cemented design, almost immediately.

Although Janet recovered well after surgery, she did experience some slight discomfort in the hip joint. She was told this was normal but five days after the procedure she suddenly developed acute, agonising discomfort when she twisted in bed.

An emergency X-ray demonstrated that she had dislocated the joint, having twisted herself into an awkward position. This required the administration of a further general anaesthetic, the hip joint being relocated.

After the relocation procedure she was asked to wear a supporting hip brace for a six-week period, the brace then being removed.

After removal of the brace, Janet noticed there was still slight discomfort in the artificial hip joint, but the replacement was more stable. She has now returned to full activities, albeit with mild discomfort, and has promised never to twist in bed unwisely again!

KEY POINTS

■ The hip is replaced for three main reasons: pain, deformity or to protect other joints

■ Try to maintain as high a degree of general fitness before the operation as possible

■ Complications may occur during or after surgery

■ The results of hip replacement are varied and depend on both the design used and the skill of the surgeon

Knee replacement

Why replace the knee?

As with the hip, the knee is replaced for three reasons:

1 Pain

2 Deformity

3 Protection of other joints.

Pain is the overriding reason. It is usually the last resort – conservative therapy will have failed and alternative operations decided against.

The knee with osteoarthritis is also classically deformed. More frequently bow-legged (varus), it can sometimes be knock-kneed (valgus). The valgus knee is a harder knee to replace than the varus one, because there are some very delicate nerves on the outer aspect of the knee which can sometimes be damaged when trying to correct the alignment of a valgus joint.

History of knee replacement

Knee replacement is not new. In the 1930s the operation of hemiarthroplasty (or half joint replacement) was performed. There then followed a period of replacing knees with devices that were known as constrained replacements. These were like hinges, simply allowing to-and-fro motion of the artificial knee after surgery.

However, it is now known that the normal knee not only bends and straightens, but also twists and turns. Consequently, any artificial knee, if it is to stand the test of time, should also allow some degree of rotational movement. The constrained designs, particularly in hinged form, did not do this. As a result, loosening eventually occurred. Despite this, constrained designs can still be used today, particularly for revision procedures.

Total condylar implant

In the early 1970s a design known as a total condylar implant was introduced. This involved placing a metal cap over the lower femur and a plastic surface on the tibial plateau. The plastic surface was shaped to mimic the normal tibial plateau in order to allow the joint to bend, straighten and rotate. Sometimes it was also considered desirable to leave the cruciate ligaments intact, particularly the posterior one, when a knee was replaced. This concept is still upheld today in certain hospitals.

A number of knee replacement designs also left the anterior cruciate ligament intact although these are no longer widely performed. Removing the cruciate ligament is not as bad as it sounds. A knee replacement without cruciate ligaments is usually better than an arthritic knee with cruciates.

The artificial components are also designed to take into account the lack of cruciates. For example, a small stud can be placed in the centre of the tibial component to compensate for the lack of a posterior cruciate,

Total condylar knee replacement

The total condylar implant has now become the benchmark prosthesis for knee replacement.

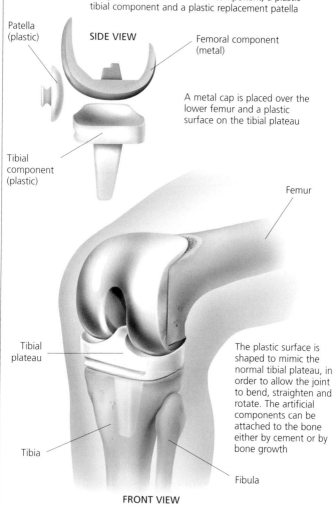

The total condylar implant comprises two or three components: a metal femoral component, a plastic tibial component and a plastic replacement patella

Patella (plastic)

SIDE VIEW

Femoral component (metal)

A metal cap is placed over the lower femur and a plastic surface on the tibial plateau

Tibial component (plastic)

Femur

Tibial plateau

The plastic surface is shaped to mimic the normal tibial plateau, in order to allow the joint to bend, straighten and rotate. The artificial components can be attached to the bone either by cement or by bone growth

Tibia

Fibula

FRONT VIEW

while the plastic is also scooped out slightly to provide better stability for the femoral component as it flexes and extends.

The total condylar implant has now become the benchmark prosthesis for knee replacements worldwide. However, surgeons remain divided in their opinions about whether or not the posterior cruciate ligament should be conserved or sacrificed during surgery.

Cement vs cementless fixation

As with hip replacement, knee replacements may be cemented or cementless, referring to the type of fixation needed to attach the artificial components to the bone.

A cemented fixation involves the use of polymethyl-methacrylate cement, allowing an instant, secure attachment to the patient.

A cementless component often requires the artificial knee to be coated in special chemicals or materials (for example, hydroxyapatite) in order to encourage the patient's bone to grow into the component, thereby fixing it securely to the patient.

The advantage of a cementless design is to make revision surgery easier, if it is ever required. It is thought that cementless components are simpler to remove. In practice, this is not always the case. Cementless designs can sometimes be very difficult to exchange at revision surgery because the patient's bone can grow tightly into the artificial component.

Unicompartmental replacement

Sometimes surgeons consider that replacement of the whole knee is unnecessary. For example, with osteoarthritis affecting only the inner part of the joint, why replace the outer part of the knee at all?

There is logic in this argument and, for this reason, the unicompartmental knee replacement was created. This involves replacing either the inner or the outer half of the knee, leaving the undamaged part of the joint alone.

Unicompartmental replacement is a good option, provided that careful selection of patients is undertaken beforehand. The arthritis must be truly located to one part of the knee.

If there is any risk of the arthritis being more generalised within the joint, surgeons often decide to perform a total rather than a unicompartmental replacement.

Patellectomy

Some patients develop their osteoarthritis in the front of the knee only. This can be an agonising condition. The most common treatment is the operation of patellectomy, removing the patella or kneecap.

However, in certain hospitals replacement of the patellofemoral joint (the joint between the kneecap and the thigh bone) is undertaken. Patellofemoral joint replacements do not always have the same success as total knee replacements and are thus not undertaken by everyone.

Patellectomy is often considered to be a safer option, perhaps being more predictable. However, when a patella is removed there can be some weakening of the knee's strength. The choice between the two is sometimes a difficult one.

Preparing for the operation

Patients can do several things to help themselves recover quickly from the operation including the items in the box on page 78.

It is also sensible to prepare for after the operation. Once at home, the patient may find that it is sometimes difficult to bend the knee fully, despite an excellent joint replacement. Most replacements flex to little more than a right angle after surgery. For this reason it may be difficult to sit in low chairs, to walk up and down stairs nimbly, or to bend and squat to pick fallen items off the floor. New furniture may be necessary or it may be possible to adapt existing furniture to new needs (see 'When can I ...?', page 92, for details).

Devices are also available that make various tasks easier. This is the realm of the occupational therapist who can advise accordingly. Part of their job is to ensure that you can carry out your normal daily life as easily as possible after any operation or illness.

You can get in touch with an occupational therapist through the surgeon you are under or the ward you are in. Some devices are free of charge, whereas others need to be paid for. Most hospitals can provide a list of addresses to contact well before surgery so that appropriate plans can be made, and devices obtained.

The operation

As with other major surgery, the patient has to be assessed before the operation to make sure that they are fit for the operation. Usually a full medical history will be taken, and various tests performed as shown in the box on page 79.

Admission is either the day before or on the day of surgery. Premedication is usually provided to ensure smooth and effective anaesthesia. Surgery may be performed under either general or local anaesthetic.

Antibiotics to prevent infection and medication to reduce the chance of blood clots forming in the calf

How you can help your recovery from an operation

- Stopping smoking: smokers are more liable to have breathing complications while they are under anaesthetic, and are also more prone to chest infection after the operation. This can prolong the period of bed rest and delay a patient getting back on their feet.

- Losing weight: an overweight patient is harder to operate on than a slim one. The knee is covered with more flesh, so more flesh needs to be cut to expose the knee properly, which leads to more bleeding. It is also physically more difficult (heavier work) for the surgeons who have to manipulate the leg during surgery. Very overweight patients are also more liable to have breathing difficulties under anaesthesia. Patients should lose whatever weight they can as every pound helps. Less weight will also put less strain on the replacement.

- Drugs: prescription drugs for heart or blood pressure should be taken regularly so that the patient is as fit for the operation as possible.

- Exercise: patients should try to do whatever exercise they can manage, as the fitter they are the easier it will be to get back on their feet. The physiotherapist at the hospital can recommend exercises to strengthen specific parts of the body – for instance, the arms, so that they can support the body better after the operation.

Tests before the operation

- Blood tests to check for anaemia, and to make sure that the blood electrolytes or salts are at a normal level. Blood will also be taken for blood grouping and supplies ordered in case you need a transfusion after the operation. About a third of patients will require a blood transfusion after knee replacement.

- Urine is also tested because it is essential that no evidence of a urinary tract infection is present at the time of surgery. If this happens, there is a small chance that the knee replacement can also become infected.

- X-rays of the chest to check that there is no chest infection – which can lead to breathing difficulties during and after the operation – and to check that the heart outline is normal and the heart can withstand the operation.

- X-rays of the knee to guide the surgeons. Occasionally a CT scan may be performed.

- An ECG (electrocardiogram): a heart tracing to ensure the heart is functioning normally.

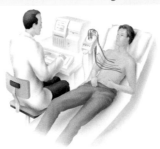

An ECG (electrocardiogram) ensures that your heart is functioning normally.

The knee replacement operation

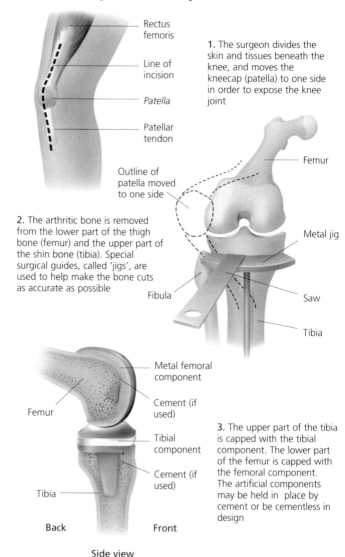

Rectus femoris

Line of incision

Patella

Patellar tendon

1. The surgeon divides the skin and tissues beneath the knee, and moves the kneecap (patella) to one side in order to expose the knee joint

Femur

Outline of patella moved to one side

Metal jig

2. The arthritic bone is removed from the lower part of the thigh bone (femur) and the upper part of the shin bone (tibia). Special surgical guides, called 'jigs', are used to help make the bone cuts as accurate as possible

Fibula

Saw

Tibia

Metal femoral component

Cement (if used)

Femur

Tibial component

Cement (if used)

Tibia

3. The upper part of the tibia is capped with the tibial component. The lower part of the femur is capped with the femoral component. The artificial components may be held in place by cement or be cementless in design

Back

Front

Side view

4. The back of the patella may also be replaced, although some surgeons elect not to do this

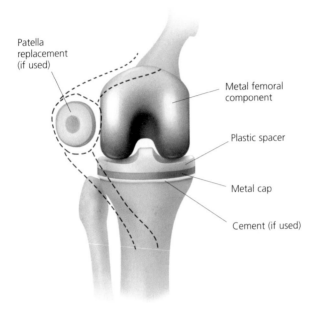

Patella replacement (if used)

Metal femoral component

Plastic spacer

Metal cap

Cement (if used)

Front view

5. The patella is then moved back to its original position and the wound is closed by stitches or clips

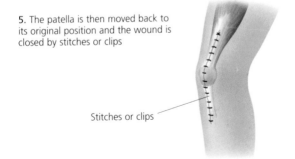

Stitches or clips

(deep vein thrombosis) may also be given, as in hip replacements. This is because, after the knee replacement, the patient will be bed-bound for a period, and clots may form as a result of a slower circulation through the legs at this stage.

The operation may involve a lengthy incision on the front of the knee, although some surgeons undertake knee replacements using smaller incisions, referred to as 'minimal incision' total knee replacement. Occasionally the skin incision is to one side of the knee. Computerised assistance may also be used by some surgeons to help with the alignment of the knee replacement components.

The success of a knee replacement depends on both the security of fixation and the eventual alignment of the knee joint. It is important for the surgeon to attempt as accurate an alignment as possible (so that the leg is straight, rather than bowed or knock-kneed).

To help in this, most knee replacement manufacturers provide instruments known as jigs. These allow the surgeon to place bone cuts accurately, in order to ensure that eventual alignment is satisfactory.

Jigs are normally made of metal and are applied to the ends or sides of the bone to act as accurate guides against which a saw can be placed. They ensure that saw cuts are straight, at the correct angles, and leave a flat surface behind against which the artificial components can be placed.

Computer-assisted operations can also be performed, using special computer programs to ensure precise placement of the components. This is sometimes called 'navigation'.

Once the operation is complete, a process that can take about one and a half hours, small plastic drains may be inserted to mop up the blood that leaks out from around the knee after surgery. The skin is closed with either clips or stitches and, once awake and comfortable, the patient returns to the ward.

Rehabilitation after surgery

Normally the patient is allowed a short period of rest. In some units, however, rehabilitation begins immediately. This is provided by the physiotherapist, in cooperation with the patient's own hard efforts.

Many units will use a continuous passive motion machine (CPM). This is a device that automatically bends and straightens the knee joint, gradually increasing the range of motion as the hours and days go by.

CPM is normally used for a set period of time each day, say four or five hours. Only occasionally is it used day and night, for 24 hours at a time.

It allows persistent movement to be applied to the postoperative knee rather than the intermittent rehabilitation that can be provided by the physiotherapist. Postoperative rehabilitation is frequently a combination of physiotherapy and CPM.

Continuous passive motion (CPM)

A continuous passive motion (CPM) device automatically bends and straightens the knee joint, gradually increasing the range of movement over time.

Walking frame

You will normally use a walking frame to assist you in the early stages of recovery.

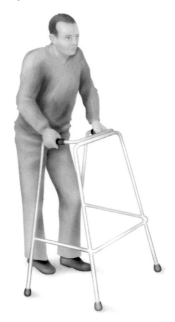

It is unlikely that a patient will walk without walking support immediately after surgery. Normally a walking frame will be provided at the beginning, followed by crutches, and then by walking stick support. Frequently, a patient can expect to be walking supported by one walking stick about six weeks after surgery.

There are, however, many variations to this regimen. In certain circumstances it may be necessary for a patient to remain non-weight-bearing (that is, no weight allowed on top of the leg) for a period after surgery.

For instance, a bone-grafting procedure might have been used at surgery if areas of bone weakening were evident, such as may occur after fractures, or even with bone tumours.

The surgeon may also wish to protect a cementless component while the bone grows into the artificial materials, in order to secure them to the patient's bone.

Complications

Although complications are infrequent, it is an unfortunate fact that they can occur. They can be divided into two categories: those that occur as a result of surgery in general (general complications) and those that are particular to knee replacements (specific complications)

General complications
Infection (two to five per cent)
This will often be treated with strong antibiotics. There is occasional need to reoperate. Sometimes reoperation is performed in more than one stage. This is called a two-stage revision.

Haematoma (or large bruise) formation at the wound
Occasionally the blood collected in the bruise has to be removed by opening the wound again.

Wound dehiscence
This means that the wound splits open again and has to be restitched.

Entrapped drain (very rare)
Occasionally the small plastic drain becomes stuck and a further operation is required to remove it.

Urinary complications (up to 35 per cent)

It is quite common for patients to have difficulty passing urine after surgery and this is most probably the result of the difficulty of passing urine when still in bed. Occasionally the use of a local, spinal anaesthetic can result in retention of urine, but this is not as common as many think. For this reason a small tube (catheter) can be passed into the bladder to assist urination for a few days.

Cardiovascular complications (up to 60 per cent)

Surgical stress can sometimes be so great that a heart attack can occur, although this happens in less than half a per cent of patients. Occasionally a blood clot can form on the brain to give rise to a stroke.

Deep vein thrombosis (DVT) and pulmonary embolism (PE)

A DVT (deep vein thrombosis) is a blood clot that forms, usually in one of the deep veins in the leg. One of the most common situations in which a DVT can form is during an operation, especially during hip and knee surgery. This is because the blood flow through the legs is sluggish when a patient is immobile and so the blood is more likely to clot.

Occasionally part of the blood clot breaks off and travels in the blood to the lungs. This is called a pulmonary embolus (PE) and in some cases can be fatal. Because of these risks patients may be given blood-thinning drugs (anticoagulants) and other measures such as special support stockings to wear to help prevent a blood clot forming.

Breathing complications

These occur mainly as a result of the anaesthetic and the bed rest. Patients with previous chest or heart problems may be more prone to this.

Death (about one per cent)

This can be for a variety of reasons – usually related to breathing or heart complications that develop during the operation.

Specific complications

Loosening (eight per cent, ten years after surgery)

This figure was obtained from an American study looking at more than 12,000 knee replacements. If symptoms of loosening become too severe then revision may be needed.

Bone fracture (two per cent)

This is as a result of longer-standing knee replacements, associated with bone weakening. As with hip replacements, the metal-on-polyethylene articulation can produce small quantities of plastic debris which can, in turn, result in osteolysis (softening and destruction of bone). Fracture can occasionally occur at operation, although more commonly some time afterwards as a result of gradual osteolysis. Reoperation is often required should this happen.

Instability (two per cent)

It has already been shown how important ligaments are to the stability of a knee joint. The knee is not a ball and socket like the hip, where the shape of the joint provides inherent stability. After knee replacement ligaments can sometimes be floppier than is desirable, causing the joint to click and clunk. When mild, this is not a problem. Sometimes further surgery is required to rectify the situation if it becomes too troublesome.

Patellar dislocation (one per cent)

The patella (kneecap) can sometimes dislocate after surgery. Normally surgeons will attempt to recognise this problem at the time of the operation, and may then perform a procedure known as a lateral release. This is a division of the tissues along the outer aspect of the kneecap, reducing the tendency for the small bone to dislocate sideways.

Failure of wound healing (less than five per cent)

Knee replacement involves implantation of synthetic materials very close to the skin. It is therefore possible that the wound can fail to heal. If this happens, the delayed healing can act as a track along which infection can travel. It is important that the wound is kept as clean as possible while healing occurs.

Altered feeling over the knee (up to 100 per cent)

It is normal for patients after knee replacement to lose some feeling over the outer part of the knee. This is not a functional problem and is a reflection of the way in which the skin's nerve supply is distributed.

Results from knee replacement

It is difficult to generalise about the results of knee replacement because there are so many different designs. The hinged, constrained designs behave in a different manner to the total condylar.

However, for a hinged knee replacement, about 75 per cent function reasonably six years after surgery, although infection rates have been as high as 13 per cent in some surveys.

Total condylar replacements demonstrate more than 92 per cent performing well 12 years after surgery. These results apply to the cemented designs. Cementless designs show 93 per cent success at five years, whereas results for longer-term studies are still awaited.

Revision knee replacement is very different. About 80 per cent can be expected to work reasonably well about three years after surgery, although infection rates can be as high as 19 per cent.

Unicompartmental knee replacements demonstrate 80 per cent performing satisfactorily 10 years after surgery.

Case report: Susan

Susan was once a keen amateur tennis player. However, a succession of injuries to her right knee, culminating in damage to her anterior cruciate ligament, had resulted in premature osteoarthritis developing.

At the age of 58 years she found that the osteoarthritis largely affected the inner part of the knee joint. The leg was becoming somewhat bowed; her orthopaedic surgeon recommended that she underwent a knee replacement.

She was worried about this, although was also aware that a tibial osteotomy (in which the shin bone is cut and rejoined in an effort to relieve pain) would not necessarily cure her discomfort. She therefore accepted the recommendation that a unicompartmental knee replacement should be given and was admitted to hospital for the procedure.

The surgery took 45 minutes, involving the implantation of a small metal runner on the lower end of her inner femur and a small plastic liner on the upper end of her inner tibia. Within seven days she was bending the knee to well over a right angle and was free of arthritis pain.

She did notice some stiffness and swelling, but this had settled within three months of the operation. She is now delighted that she underwent surgery, although she has accepted that she will be unable to return to her sporting life.

Her surgeon has insisted that she takes life gently, to protect the artificial components, and has explained that one day Susan may require conversion of her unicompartmental knee replacement to a total condylar design.

Case report: Sam

Sam has a very chequered history of left knee problems. Twenty years ago he underwent a constrained (hinged) knee replacement for gross osteoarthritis of the knee joint. Initially this worked well, though he did notice some restriction of movement.

Eight years after surgery he began to experience discomfort, his surgeon explaining that the replacement was beginning to work loose. He demonstrated to Sam the bone thinning that was beginning to appear on X-ray. Sam therefore underwent a revision operation. The constrained components were removed, replaced by yet further components and bone graft.

He was asked to remain non-weight-bearing for three months after the procedure while the bone graft was incorporated. After this operation the X-ray looked much better and Sam's symptoms were much improved.

Nevertheless, pain returned five years later, and the surgeon explained how difficult it was to make a revision operation last as long as the initial replacement.

Sam has struggled on since that last consultation, but realises a further operation is going to be required. This will be more complex than the previous one. He understands that the problem was created by having a knee replacement at a relatively young age.

Sam now understands that synthetic devices do not always last forever and that his knee problems are not over yet.

KEY POINTS

■ The knee can be replaced for three reasons: pain, deformity or to protect other joints

■ The total condylar implant is now the benchmark prosthesis for knee replacements world wide

■ Complications can occur at, or after, knee replacement operations

■ Of total condylar replacements, 92 per cent perform well for at least 12 years after surgery

When can I ...?

Frequently asked questions

Surgery is a natural worry for most patients. However, for many it is what happens after the operation that is most important; this is particularly so for procedures such as hip or knee replacement when the aim is to return a patient to a quality of life that has long ago disappeared.

Hip and knee replacements have certain features in common. As the diameter of the components is so much larger than for most hip replacements, hip resurfacing operations have a lesser chance of dislocation, so some surgeons allow more leeway with resurfacings than with hip replacements after surgery. Frequently asked questions are as follows.

But note well ...

With all these questions, the answer may vary from surgeon to surgeon. There is an increasing trend now to limit the amount that a patient is restricted after a joint replacement. For example, some surgeons will allow their patients to sleep on their side earlier than others, some are not so rigid about sitting in low chairs, and so on.

It is important that you ask your own surgeon how he or she wishes patients to behave after a joint replacement. See the answers given below as a guide.

When can I return to work?

It depends on your job. For most sedentary activities a return to work at six weeks after surgery is reasonable. For more active jobs a minimum of three months is required.

When can I play sports?

It depends on the sport. Contact sports are best avoided altogether after joint replacement surgery, although they are permissible approximately four weeks after arthroscopic (keyhole) procedures on the knee and up to four months after arthroscopic procedures on the hip.

Non-contact activities (for example, golf) are fine a minimum of six weeks after joint replacement, although more preferably at three months. Some surgeons advise that sports such as tennis are best avoided after joint replacement, though doubles, at a gentler pace, would be permissible.

When can I have sex?

What is stopping you? After knee replacement no holds should be barred. After hip replacement you must be careful not to flex your hip to more than 90 degrees. Be as inventive as you wish, but keep this simple rule in mind.

When can I drive a car?

Six weeks is a safe bet after hip or knee replacement.

Most car seats are fairly low, putting the hip replacement at risk of dislocation.

Also knees should be able to flex to at least a right angle to make driving reasonably comfortable. This can take anything up to six weeks. When you do drive a car, put the seat as far back as is safe and incline the back rest towards the rear very slightly.

When can I ride a horse or bicycle?

Some surgeons advise that both horse and bicycle riding should be avoided after hip or knee replacement. Not everyone agrees. Both activities are sometimes reasonable, though three months after surgery is a safe period to wait.

When can I stop using my crutches?

The physiotherapist will advise about this. However, most patients will stop using crutches between two and three weeks after hip or knee replacement. For those needing extra care and caution, crutches may be required for six weeks, and occasionally for three months. Once crutch use has stopped, a walking stick is advised for a period.

When can I stop using my deep vein thrombosis (DVT) stockings?

It is quite common for patients to be provided support stockings while in hospital. These, combined with a variety of medications, can reduce the chances of DVT formation.

Six weeks is a normal period for such stockings to be worn, but in hot weather they can occasionally be itchy. Your surgeon will advise, but it is sometimes possible to stop using them earlier than the six-week period.

When can I lie on my side?

Whenever you wish after knee replacement. Following hip replacement it is best to avoid lying on your side for six weeks. In particular, the operated side should not be uppermost.

Many people sleep curled up into a little ball. If the upper leg flops downwards onto the bed in the curled position, the hip can dislocate. This risk does not apply to hip resurfacings.

When can I sit on a low chair?

After hip replacement, never! Chairs need to be at least 19 inches (48 centimetres) high to be safe. Why not mark this level on your walking stick so that you can instantly identify safe chairs on which to sit?

You should also ensure that chairs have armrests to allow you to stand up and sit down easily. This guideline does not apply to hip resurfacings, where the chance of a dislocation is tiny.

Chairs of any height may be used, as long as the hip feels comfortable. After knee replacement there is no limit to the height of chair as a knee is most unlikely to dislocate. Nevertheless, the 19-inch rule is more comfortable as this will ensure that the knee joint is not bent too much.

When can I go swimming?

Once the wound has healed after a knee replacement, but three months after hip replacement. The breast stroke is a particularly worrisome stroke. This places a twisting force on both the hip and the knee. You can do it after hip or knee replacement, but do swim very carefully indeed.

When can I put on my own shoes, socks and stockings? For that matter when can I cut my own toenails?

Three months after the operation. In order to reach as far down as your feet and toes, your hip joint must flex perilously near to 90 degrees. After knee replacement, you can perform the above activities as soon as you wish.

When can I climb stairs?

As soon as you are happy to do so. It is sometimes difficult with two crutches, particularly if your surgeon asks you to remain non-weight-bearing. However, there is no mechanical reason why you should not climb stairs from the moment you return home, if you can manage them.

When can I carry weights/do the shopping?

I would wait at least six weeks after surgery. It is difficult to carry weights when you are also having to use crutches or two walking sticks.

When can I climb in and out of the bath?

As soon as you can bend your knee sufficiently well to do the job and, of course, as soon as the wound is well enough healed to withstand a good soaking – two weeks minimum would be reasonable.

Common worries and concerns

Surgery is a worrying time for all patients. Such feelings are perfectly natural. Many individuals, quite unnecessarily, feel that to ask questions is silly. This is not the case.

It is natural to want to know as much as possible about one's operation. It is the surgeon's job to answer any queries put forward as clearly and as fully as possible. Common worries and concerns may be as follows.

Why this particular design?
There are countless designs available for hip and knee replacement operations. What is important is that any design chosen should have a proven track record. Some designs have appeared with a fanfare of trumpets, only to disappear six months later.

What is important is that your surgeon is familiar and happy with the design of joint replacement chosen. Ask about the short- and long-term results for the chosen replacement. Do not be swayed by brief newspaper articles declaring that a given replacement is the answer to all our prayers. It may be so, but could easily vanish within a few months.

A recent hip replacement was withdrawn from the market, amid much media coverage, partly as a result of the nature of its design and partly as a result of the material from which it was made.

Titanium was believed to be part of the problem. In reality there are certain hip replacements in use today that are made of titanium, and which are lasting extremely well.

This shows how important it is to listen to the advice of your surgeon, who should be familiar with the ups and downs of the particular design chosen for you.

My wound feels warm. Is this normal?

Healing takes place after surgery and is associated with inflammation. It is therefore perfectly normal for a wound to feel warm for a period, particularly so for knee replacements where the artificial components are only a hair's breadth below the skin surface.

Warmth of the wound is normal for at least six months after surgery and does not necessarily mean anything is untoward. Increasing warmth can sometimes be a problem and should be brought to your surgeon's attention.

I seem to be numb around my scar. Is this a problem?

No problem at all. Most patients after knee replacement will be numb over the outer aspect of the knee. Many patients after hip replacement will also be numb over a small area behind the scar. These observations are generally of no functional significance whatsoever.

Is it a problem that my leg is swollen after surgery?

Sometimes yes, sometimes no. Until an individual is walking fully and normally, the muscle pump does not drive blood back to the heart as effectively as it could. Consequently it is normal for a leg to swell, particularly on the operated side.

However, leg swelling can also be an indication of deep vein thrombosis (DVT). If swelling is associated with discomfort, it should be brought to your surgeon's attention immediately. Leg swelling should have disappeared three months after surgery, preferably earlier.

My joint replacement is persistently painful. Should I worry?

It is quite common for patients to say that their joint replacement, be it hip or knee, aches after surgery. The aching is different to the intense agony of arthritis felt before the procedure.

However, the discomfort should be very mild and should not increase. If it does, please ask your surgeon. It is possible that the replacement is loosening, or infection is setting in. The chances of these are extremely small, but it is better to be safe than sorry.

My joint does not bend as well after replacement as it did before. Is this a problem?

Not usually. After hip replacement it is normal to advise a patient not to flex the joint to more than 90 degrees. This is in order to prevent joint dislocation. After knee replacement, it is usual for the joint to be able to bend to slightly more than a right angle.

It is unusual to regain full, natural movement after knee replacement. Occasionally, gross stiffness can set in after hip or knee replacement. If this happens, your surgeon should be consulted.

My joint replacement clicks and clunks. Should I worry?

Not usually. It is quite normal for a knee replacement to gently click and clunk when the knee is moved, particularly from side to side. These feelings reflect the gentle thumping of the plastic tibial component on the metal femoral component.

They are common in the early postoperative days, but should lessen significantly within a six- to eight-week period. Clicking and clunking from the hip are unusual. This is normally a feature of slackness of the joint and should again disappear as the muscles tighten up following surgery.

Occasionally it can be a reflection of hip instability and may herald dislocation. You should therefore advise your surgeon if your hip or knee replacement clicks or clunks after operation.

Will I need to make many changes to my home?

Probably not. However, it would be worth ensuring that you have banisters on your stairs, and rails at convenient points near the bath and loo.

You should have at least one chair in your living room, the seat of which is at least 19 inches (48 cm) from the floor, with a straight backrest and with two arms that you can use to help you sit down and rise to your feet.

Beds can be raised by blocks in the early stages after replacement surgery, rather than going to the expense of buying a new bed. Your occupational therapist can advise.

Case report: Martina

Martina, aged 67, had osteoarthritis, but was keen to return to hill walking, which she loved. She had accepted that she would never be able to walk quite as far as she had in previous years, but a knee replacement seemed the best option.

However, 10 weeks after surgery, despite copious physiotherapy, she was able to bend the knee only to 45 degrees. This concerned her. She reported her worries to her surgeon who advised that 45 degrees was less than he would ideally wish to see at such a stage, but she should continue with physiotherapy for a further 4 weeks.

She did so, being able to bend to 60 degrees by the time she reattended for her next outpatient review; 60 degrees was still not enough, so her surgeon admitted her to undertake a manipulation of the knee under general anaesthetic.

With Martina asleep he gently bent the knee to 120 degrees. He could feel the clicks and clunks of the scar tissue breaking down as he did this. When Martina awoke her knee was somewhat painful, but the discomfort rapidly settled.

The manipulation was followed by a five-day period of continuous passive motion machine usage. By the time she was discharged from hospital, Martina was able to bend her knee freely to 120 degrees and has now returned to gentle hill rambling.

KEY POINTS

■ It is perfectly natural to have worries and questions about your operation

■ Ask your surgeon about any queries that you have before the operation

Exercises after hip or knee arthritis surgery

However well a surgeon may perform an operation, much work still remains to be done after surgery. This is the domain of the physiotherapist (who is concerned with helping someone regain their physical strength and mobility after an operation or illness) and occupational therapist (who is concerned with helping patients to carry out daily activities in and out of the home).

Full rehabilitation, however, is not possible without concerted effort from the patient. Rehabilitation and exercises can be divided into two categories:

1 Early postoperative and bed exercises
2 Exercises to be done once the patient is able to sit in a chair or to walk.

Exercises to do after a knee replacement
Early postoperative and bed exercises

These exercises should be performed whenever the patient is in bed, and most certainly in the first week after surgery. Exercises 1–5 should be undertaken 10 times every 30 minutes. Exercises 6 and 7 may be performed every hour.

Sit with your back supported at an angle of 45 degrees, legs straight out in front of you. Now do the following:

1 Keeping your legs straight on the bed, pull your foot up, pointing your toes to the ceiling and keeping your knees straight. Then point your toes and foot down towards the end of the bed. Do this each way as far as possible.

2 In the same position, circle both feet round at the ankle in each direction.

3 Squeeze your buttock muscles tightly together, then relax them.

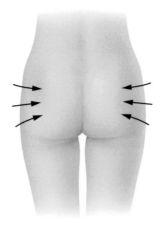

4   Brace your knees straight by tightening the
    quadriceps (thigh) muscles, pushing the leg down
    hard on the bed.

5   Gently bend your knee to an angle of no more than
    45 degrees, then lower slowly. You may use your
    hands to help you. This exercise may be easier if the
    physiotherapist provides a sliding board. This is a
    smooth piece of wood or plastic that goes under
    the heel, to allow the heel to slide on the sheets.
    Without it the heel might catch on the bedclothes
    and movement would be difficult, if not impossible.

6 Place a rolled-up towel under the knee to make it bend slightly. Then point your toes to the ceiling, tighten the quadriceps muscles and raise your foot and heel off the bed. Make sure your knee is straight, count to ten, then lower your foot slowly and relax.

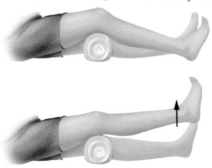

7 Tighten your quadriceps muscle, point your toes to the ceiling, and raise the whole leg off the bed at least 6 inches (15 centimetres). Lower the leg slowly to the bed once again and relax. This is called a straight leg raise. Watch your knee as the leg lifts. It should lift as one, without any bend of the joint, when it first comes off the bed. If any bend occurs, however minor, this is referred to as lag. You should attempt to eliminate lag as soon as possible after surgery.

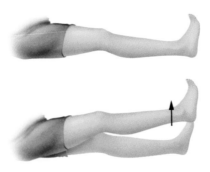

Exercises to do when you are able to sit in a chair or walk

8 Lie on your stomach. Bend one knee at a time, trying to make the heel touch the buttock. If the knee is stiff, try to help it bend with the other leg until you feel a mild stretch. Once you can bend the leg that was operated on independently, use the other leg to provide gentle resistance – do this by crossing your legs, unoperated side on top, and allow it to provide resistance as you bend the operated side.

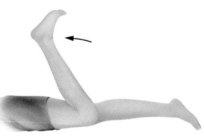

9 Sit on a chair with your knees bent, both feet firmly on the floor. Tighten the quadriceps muscle in the operated leg and raise the foot until your leg is completely straight. Then slowly lower and relax.

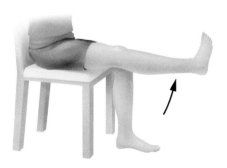

10 Still seated on a chair, bend the knee back as far as possible until you feel a gentle stretch over the front of the knee. Hold this position to the count of five, then relax. If the knee is stiff, help it by using the other leg to assist the bending action, by crossing your legs at the ankles. Do not cross your legs at the level of the calves. Once the leg that was operated on can bend independently, use the other side to apply gentle resistance against it. It is good for the operated leg to work slightly against pressure.

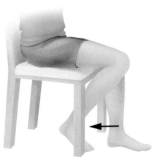

Exercises to do after a hip replacement or resurfacing
Early postoperative and bed exercises

1 With the legs straight, pull your foot up towards you until your toes are pointing to the ceiling. Then point your toes and feet down towards the end of the bed. Stretch your feet and toes each way as far as possible.

2 Circle both feet round in each direction.

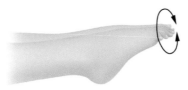

3 Tighten the muscles in both your thighs, pushing your knees down firmly into the bed.

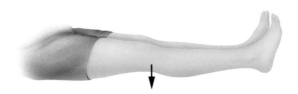

4   Squeeze your buttock muscles tightly together, then relax.

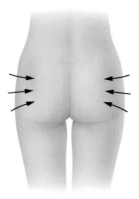

5   Bend your hip and knee gently upwards, then lower slowly. Do not pull your leg up by hand. Do not bend the hip joint to more than a right angle. It may be necessary to use a sliding board to assist with this exercise.

6   Lay your legs straight out in front of you, then tighten the muscles and slide your leg towards the edge of the bed and back again. Do not move the leg across an imaginary line running down the centre of your body, do not roll your leg outwards and keep your toes pointed towards the ceiling throughout.

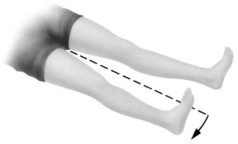

7   Place a rolled-up towel under your knee. Straighten
    your leg, tensing the muscles so that your heel lifts
    up off the bed, keeping the back of your knee in
    contact with the towel at all times. Lower your heel
    slowly back to rest on the bed.

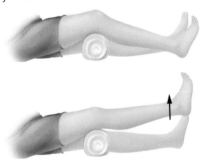

**Exercises to do when you are able to sit in a
chair or walk**
These exercises should be performed only when you
are able to sit or stand independently.

Sitting
1   Sitting on a high chair, slide your bottom to the
    front of the chair. Both feet should be firmly placed
    on the floor and take great care not to bend the
    hip to more than 90 degrees. Straighten your leg
    and tense your muscles to raise your foot off the

floor. Keep your toes pointed up towards the ceiling and hold the position for five seconds. Then lower your leg carefully towards the floor.

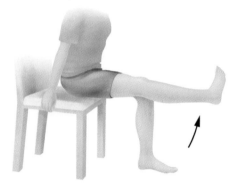

2   Adopt the same position as in exercise 1 above. Lean against the back of the chair and gently lift up your thigh, raising your foot from the floor and keeping your knee bent. Do not flex your hip

through more than a right angle. Then lower your leg, putting your foot back on the floor. Do not pull your leg up with your hands.

Standing

The following exercises are for the operated leg only. You should stand straight, though it may be necessary to hold onto something to balance. The upper body should not be moved and the foot of the operated leg should not touch the floor during these exercises.

1 Keeping your leg straight, slowly swing your leg forwards and backwards, leaning ever so slightly to the opposite side so that it can swing without touching the floor.

2 Swing your leg sideways away from the body and then back to the centre. Keep your kneecap facing forwards at all times and do not cross your legs.

3 Swing your leg gently round in a circle – front, side, behind and return.

4 Swing your leg forwards to an angle of 45 degrees
   from the vertical and hold that position for a count
   of five. Then lower your leg and swing it gently
   back as far as possible. Hold that position for a
   count of five and then lower.

5 Swing your leg out to the side at an angle of 45 degrees from the vertical and hold it there for a count of five. Then lower. Do not let your leg come further back in than the centre of your body and keep your upper body still.

Do's and don'ts of replacement surgery

For both knee and hip joints and resurfacing

DO'S

- Do exercise regularly – gentle exercises are best

- Do increase the distance that you walk gently after surgery. There are no prizes for trying to beat the world land speed record

- Do wait between 6 and 12 weeks before you take to driving a car again after your operation

- Do wait between 6 and 12 weeks before you recommence general household activities

- Do attempt sexual intercourse any time!

- Do begin hobbies such as gardening, bowls, and swimming 6 to 12 weeks after surgery. For more active pastimes you should wait until the 12-week point for sure

DON'TS

- Don't cross your legs. This is bad for circulation

- Don't allow yourself to become overtired.

- Don't sit on low stools, chairs or toilets (not applicable to hip resurfacings)

- Don't sit on chairs without arms

- Don't get up from a chair without first moving to the front edge of it

- Don't try to put on your own shoes, socks or stockings without the help of a special appliance

- Don't jump

Do's and don'ts of replacement surgery (contd)

DON'TS (contd)

- Don't pick up objects from the floor without placing the operated leg straight behind you

- Don't do any heavy lifting

- Don't overeat – it is important that you don't become overweight

Specific, extra precautions after hip replacement surgery

- Do not cross your legs (except at the ankles)

- Do not bend the hip beyond a right angle (90 degrees)

- Do not twist the hip inwards or outwards

- Do not pivot on the operated leg

- Do not stretch forwards from a sitting position

Tricks of the trade

Your physiotherapist will advise the best way of approaching many routine, daily activities. However, getting out of a chair, and in and out of a car, are frequently asked questions. The basic principle is to use arm rests when you can and to place the operated leg out in front of you when rising out of, or sitting down on, a chair.

The same principle applies to getting in and out of a car. Again, you must slide your bottom as far back into the car as you can, keeping the operated leg straight out in front of you. Swing the leg round at the last moment once you have pushed your bottom as far back into the seat as you can.

Getting in and out of a bath is a similar performance. Make certain that you have assistance to hand when you first try this and climb into the bath from a standing stool at first. You should have handrails fitted, if the bath is not already provided with them.

Take care not to pivot on the operated leg and avoid bending the hip to a right angle. Use a bath seat at first as well. Step into the bath directly from the side, leading with the unoperated leg.

Once you are standing with both legs in the bath shuffle around to face the front end. Then reach back for the handrail, keeping the operated leg straight out in front.

A rubber bath mat is useful to give some grip. Slowly lower yourself onto the bath seat and start washing! Reverse the procedure to get out.

KEY POINTS

- Full rehabilitation after surgery requires a concerted effort from the patient

- Exercise regularly but gently

- Do not sit on chairs that have no armrests

- Avoid putting on any weight

Useful addresses

We have included the following organisations because,
on preliminary investigation, they may be of use to the
reader. However, we do not have first-hand experience
of each organisation and so cannot guarantee the
organisation's integrity. The reader must therefore
exercise his or her own discretion and judgement when
making further enquiries.

Arthritis Care
18 Stephenson Way
London NW1 2HD
Tel: 020 7380 6500
Information line: 0845 600 6868
Freephone: 0808 800 4050 (12 noon–4pm Mon–Fri)
Source helpline (for those under 26): 0808 808 2000
(10am–4pm Mon–Fri)
Website: www.arthritiscare.org.uk

Provides information, advice and practical aid to people
with arthritis. Has branches throughout the country
and publishes a bi-monthly paper, Arthritis News, for

its members, and has network of local branches and support groups. Runs self-management training courses and has four specially adapted hotels.

Arthritis Research Campaign
Copeman House, St Mary's Court
St Mary's Gate
Chesterfield S41 7TD
Tel: 0870 850 5000
Website: www.arc.org.uk

Finances an extensive programme of research and education and produces over 80 helpful booklets, available from the ARC, your GP or your rheumatologist. Publishes a quarterly magazine, Arthritis Today, for the general public.

Benefits Enquiry Line
Tel: 0800 882200
Minicom: 0800 243355
Website: www.dwp.gov.uk
N. Ireland: 0800 220674

Government agency giving information and advice on sickness and disability benefits for people with disabilities and their carers.

Clinical Knowledge Summaries
Sowerby Centre for Health Informatics at Newcastle
(SCHIN Ltd), Bede House, All Saints Business Centre
Newcastle upon Tyne NE1 2ES
Tel: 0191 243 6100
Website: www.cks.library.nhs.uk

A website mainly for GPs giving information for patients listed by disease plus named self-help organisations.

Disabled Living Foundation
380–384 Harrow Road
London W9 2HU
Tel: 020 7289 6111
Helpline: 0845 130 9177 (Mon–Fri 10am–4pm)
Textphone: 020 7432 8009 (Mon–Fri 10am–4pm)
Website: www.dlf.org.uk

Provides information to disabled and elderly people on all kinds of equipment in order to promote their independence and quality of life.

DVLA (Driver and Vehicle Licensing Agency)
DVLA
Swansea SA99 1TU
Tel: 0870 600 0301
Website: www.dvla.gov.uk

Provides advice and information leaflets about hip and knee surgery and driving.

National Institute for Health and Clinical Excellence (NICE)
MidCity Place, 71 High Holborn
London WC1V 6NA
Tel: 0845 003 7780
Website: www.nice.org.uk

Provides national guidance on the promotion of good health and the prevention and treatment of ill health.

Patient information leaflets are available for each piece of guidance issued.

NHS Direct

Tel: 0845 4647 (24 hours, 365 days a year)
Website: www.nhsdirect.nhs.uk

Offers confidential health-care advice, information and referral service. A good first port of call for any health advice.

NHS Smoking Helpline

Freephone: 0800 022 4332 (7am–11pm, 365 days a year)
Website: www.gosmokefree.nhs.uk
Pregnancy smoking helpline: 0800 169 9169
(7am–11pm, 365 days a year)

Have advice, help and encouragement on giving up smoking. Specialist advisers available to offer ongoing support to those who genuinely are trying to give up smoking. Can refer to local branches.

Patients' Association

PO Box 935
Harrow
Middx HA1 3YJ
Tel: 020 8423 9111
Helpline: 0845 608 4455
Website: www.patients-association.com

Charity representing patients' concerns. Offers numerous publications covering a variety of areas such as how to access your medical records, and living wills (advanced directives). Also has extensive database of other useful organisations; available on request or can be downloaded from the internet.

Quit (Smoking Quitlines)

211 Old Street
London EC1V 9NR
Tel: 020 7251 1551
Helpline: 0800 002200 (9am–9pm, 365 days a year)
Website: www.quit.org.uk
Scotland: 0800 848484
Wales: 0800 169 0169 (NHS)

Offers individual advice on giving up smoking in English and Asian languages. Talks to schools on smoking and can refer to local support groups. Runs training courses for professionals.

Weight Watchers

Millennium House, Ludlow Road
Maidenhead SL6 2SL
Tel: 0845 345 1500
Website: www.weightwatchers.co.uk

Runs informal, yet structured, weekly meetings across the UK for people wanting to lose weight and learn more about living a healthy lifestyle. Guidance also available free with online programme.

Useful websites
BBC
www.bbc.co.uk/health
A helpful website: easy to navigate and offers lots of

useful advice and information. Also contains links to other related topics.

Patient UK
www.patient.co.uk

Further reading

Knee Problems: A patient's guide to treatment and recovery. By Richard Villar. London: HarperCollins.

Heal Your Hips: How to prevent hip surgery – and what to do if you need it. By Robert Klapper and Lynda Huey. Chichester: John Wiley & Sons.

The internet as a source of further information

After reading this book, you may feel that you would like further information on the subject. The internet is of course an excellent place to look and there are many websites with useful information about medical disorders, related charities and support groups.

For those who do not have a computer at home some bars and cafes offer facilities for accessing the internet. These are listed in the *Yellow Pages* under 'Internet Bars and Cafes' and 'Internet Providers'. Your local library offers a similar facility and has staff to help you find the information that you need.

It should always be remembered, however, that the internet is unregulated and anyone is free to set up a website and add information to it. Many websites offer impartial advice and information that have been compiled and checked by qualified medical professionals. Some, on the other hand, are run by commercial organisations with the purpose of promoting their own products.

Others still are run by pressure groups, some of which will provide carefully assessed and accurate information whereas others may be suggesting medications or treatments that are not supported by the medical and scientific community.

Unless you know the address of the website you want to visit – for example, www.familydoctor.co.uk – you may find the following guidelines useful when searching the internet for information.

Search engines and other searchable sites

Google (www.google.co.uk) is the most popular search engine used in the UK, followed by Yahoo! (http://uk.yahoo.com) and MSN (www.msn.co.uk). Also popular are the search engines provided by Internet Service Providers such as Tiscali and other sites such as the BBC site (www.bbc.co.uk).

In addition to the search engines that index the whole web, there are also medical sites with search facilities, which act almost like mini-search engines, but cover only medical topics or even a particular area of medicine. Again, it is wise to look at who is responsible for compiling the information offered to ensure that it is impartial and medically accurate. The NHS Direct site (www.nhsdirect.nhs.uk) is an example of a searchable medical site.

Links to many British medical charities can be found at the Association of Medical Research Charities' website (www.amrc.org.uk) and at Charity Choice (www.charitychoice.co.uk).

Search phrases

Be specific when entering a search phrase. Searching for information on 'cancer' will return results for many different types of cancer as well as on cancer in general. You may even find sites offering astrological information. More useful results will be returned by using search phrases such as 'lung cancer' and 'treatments for lung cancer'. Both Google and Yahoo! offer an advanced search option that includes the ability to search for the exact phrase; enclosing the search phrase in quotes, that is, 'treatments for lung cancer', will have the same effect. Limiting a search to an exact phrase reduces the number of results returned but it is best to refine a search to an exact match only if you are not getting useful results with a normal search. Adding 'UK' to your search term will bring up mainly British sites, so a good phrase might be 'lung cancer' UK (don't include UK within the quotes).

Always remember that the internet is international and unregulated. It holds a wealth of valuable information but individual sites may be biased, out of date or just plain wrong. Family Doctor Publications accepts no responsibility for the content of links published in this series.

Index

Your pages

We have included the following pages because they may help you manage your illness or condition and its treatment.

Before an appointment with a health professional, it can be useful to write down a short list of questions of things that you do not understand, so that you can make sure that you do not forget anything.

Some of the sections may not be relevant to your circumstances.

We are always pleased to receive constructive criticism or suggestions about how to improve the books. You can contact us at:

Email: familydoctor@btinternet.com
Letter: Family Doctor Publications
         PO Box 4664
         Poole
         BH15 1NN

Thank you

Health-care contact details

Name:

Job title:

Place of work:

Tel:

Name:

Job title:

Place of work:

Tel:

Name:

Job title:

Place of work:

Tel:

Name:

Job title:

Place of work:

Tel:

Significant past health events – illnesses/ operations/investigations/treatments

Event	Month	Year	Age (at time)

Appointments for health care

Name:

Place:

Date:

Time:

Tel:

Name:

Place:

Date:

Time:

Tel:

Name:

Place:

Date:

Time:

Tel:

Name:

Place:

Date:

Time:

Tel:

Appointments for health care

Name:

Place:

Date:

Time:

Tel:

Name:

Place:

Date:

Time:

Tel:

Name:

Place:

Date:

Time:

Tel:

Name:

Place:

Date:

Time:

Tel:

Current medication(s) prescribed by your doctor

Medicine name:

Purpose:

Frequency & dose:

Start date:

End date:

Medicine name:

Purpose:

Frequency & dose:

Start date:

End date:

Medicine name:

Purpose:

Frequency & dose:

Start date:

End date:

Medicine name:

Purpose:

Frequency & dose:

Start date:

End date:

Other medicines/supplements you are taking, not prescribed by your doctor

Medicine/treatment:

Purpose:

Frequency & dose:

Start date:

End date:

Medicine/treatment:

Purpose:

Frequency & dose:

Start date:

End date:

Medicine/treatment:

Purpose:

Frequency & dose:

Start date:

End date:

Medicine/treatment:

Purpose:

Frequency & dose:

Start date:

End date:

Questions to ask at appointments
(Note: do bear in mind that doctors work under great time pressure, so long lists may not be helpful for either of you)

Questions to ask at appointments
(Note: do bear in mind that doctors work under great time pressure, so long lists may not be helpful for either of you)

Notes